UNDERSTANDING
ISLAM & MUSLIMS

BY
AHMAD H. SAKR

Library of Congress Catalog Card Number: 90-55605
ISBN: 0- 911119-26-4

SECOND REVISED EDITION - 2001

UNDERSTANDING ISLAM AND MUSLIMS

Ahmad H. Sakr, Ph.D.

Published by:
Foundation for Islamic Knowledge
P.O. Box 665
Lombard, Illinois 60148 (USA)
Telephone: (630) 495-4817
FAX: (630) 627-8894
Tax I.D #36-352-8916

DEDICATION

This book is dedicated to Allah Ta'ala (Almighty) for all the favors He has bestowed upon me in creating and bringing me to this world. His Love, His Mercy, His Compassion, His Forgiveness, His Graciousness, His Kindness and His Bountifulness are above any humble person like me, to be able to thank Him enough and to praise Him.

O Allah ! I am humbly dedicating this work **to You.**

O Allah ! Accept my humble work and help me disseminate the information to those who need it.

O Allah ! Make this humble work worthy **of You.**

O Allah ! Forgive my shortcomings.

O Allah ! Help me live as a Muslim and die as a Mu'min (Believer).

O Allah ! Let me be summoned on the Day of Judgment with Prophet Muhammad (pbuh), with the other Prophets, the martyrs and the noble believers. Ameen.

Understanding Islam & Muslims

TABLE OF CONTENTS

ACKNOWLEDGEMENTS

The author wishes to thank all those friends who helped in making this book available to the readers. Special thanks go to Dr. Yusuf Kamaluddin (Yao-Keng) Chang and his wife, Audrey, for their tremendous help and moral support during the last few years.

Thanks and appreciation go to the Vakil families (Abu Bakr, Usman, Farouq, Ishaq, Iqbal, and Akhtar) for their support to the author and the Foundation. May Allah bless them and bless their late parents (Umar and Amina).

Moreover, the author wishes to thank all the respected brothers and sisters who have helped previously and are still helping. Among the many are Mr. Asad Khan and his wife, Sister Azma Khan; Dr. and Mrs. Mohammed Shafi; Mr. & Mrs. Javed Habib; Mr. & Mrs. Abdul Wahab; Mr. & Mrs. Saghir Aslam; Dr. & Mrs. Nadim Daouk; Mr. Refat M. Abo Elela; Dr. & Mrs. Zeyd A. Merenkov; Dr. and Mrs. Daudur Rahman; Mr. and Mrs. Shakeel Syed; Dr. and Mrs. Maqbool Ahmad; Mr. Zia Khan and his wife Tina Khan; Dr. and Mrs. Syed A. Zahir; Dr. and Mrs. Muhammad K. Zaman; Dr. and Mrs. Mostapha Arafa; Dr. & Mrs. Samir Arafeh; Dr. M. Munir Chaudry and family; Dr. Dani Doueiri; Late Dr. F.R. Khan and his respected wife Sister Farhat Khan, may Allah (swt) bless his soul, and many more.

Special thanks and appreciations go to Sister Fawzia Akalal; Sister Sajeda Sultani and her family members; Sister Houyda Najjar Mertaban and her family members; Brother Mohammed Bilal Khan; and Brother Waseem Najmi and his wife Yasmeen; for their kind help in many areas. Also our thanks and appreciations are extended to sister Azizah Abdul Rahman of Singapore, on behalf of her late parents Aminah Bint Ahmad and Abdul Rahman bin Mohamed. May Allah (swt) be pleased with her and her late parents. Ameen.

Special thanks and appreciation to Sister Shadia Hassan and her children for their help, advice, and contributions for the love of Allah. Our prayers of Maghfirah for her husband Mr. Samir Hassan. May Allah (swt) bless his soul and make his final stay in Paradise. Ameen.

We are thankful and grateful to Mr. Muhammad El-Bdeiwi and his family for their generosity in helping this Foundation for Da'wah purposes. Our thanks also go to Mr. & Mrs. Abu Ramy Assaf.

Our thanks and appreciations go to Mr. Ammar Charani and his brother Samer Charani of MEF for their help. May Allah bless them.

Thanks and appreciations go to Mr. Khaled Obagi for his support to the Foundation on behalf of his late father and mother Aref Obagi and Nabila Al-Beik. Our thanks and appreciations also go to Mr. Ahmad Al-Khatib for his support to the Foundation on behalf of his mother Soraya, and his late father Adel Baheej Al-Khatib. Thanks and appreciations also go to Dr. Osama Haikal on behalf of his late father, Mr. Omar Haikal. May Allah be pleased with them and may Allah keep their relatives in Paradise. Ameen.

Our thanks and affections are to Brother Fathy Haggag and his family for their tremendous support to the author for all the years in California. It is only Allah (swt) Who will reward them.

Last but not least, my thanks, appreciation and love are to my wife, Zuhar Barhumi Sakr and our loving children, Sara, Hussein, his wife Dania, and their daughter Aya, Jihad and Basil as well as to my grandchildren Nada, Abdur Rahman, Ibrahim, Jenna and Hena from our daughter Sara, and their father Muhammad Nasser.

We pray to Allah (swt) to open the hearts of other friends to invest with Allah in a Sadaqah Jariyah (endowment fund) on behalf of their loving parents before it is too late. Ameen

SPECIAL PRAYERS

The author prays to Allah (swt[1]) to bless Prophet Muhammad and the family of Prophet Muhammad, (pbuh[2]) in as much as He blessed Prophet Ibrahim and the family of Prophet Ibrahim. The author also prays to Allah (swt) to bless the Khulafaa' Rashidoon (Rightly guided) and the Sahaba (Companions) of the Prophet as well as the Tabi`oon (Followers) and the Followers of the Followers till the Day of Judgment.

The author prays to Allah (swt) to reward all the `Ulama', who carried the Message of Allah and His Prophet, and who transmitted it to the new generations.

The author prays to Allah (swt) to reward his parents: his late father Al-Hajj Hussain Mustafa Sakr and his late mother Al-Hajjah Sara Ramadan Sakr for their sacrifices to their twelve children in general and to this author in specific. The author prays to Allah (swt) to reward the late brother of the author, Mr. Muhammad H. Sakr, for helping the author to get his academic education, and his late brothers Mahmood H. Sakr, and Mustafa H. Sakr for taking care of the author's responsibilities overseas.

Special prayers go to the Shaikh of the author who taught him Islam, and trained him from childhood to practice its teaching: Shaikh Muhammad `Umar Da`ooq. May Allah be pleased with him.

Special Du`a' goes to Al-Shaheed Shaikh Hassan Khalid, the late Grand Mufti of Lebanon, who had also great impact on the author's knowledge of Islam. May Allah bless his soul and make him stay in Paradise.

1[1] swt: Subhanahu Wa Ta'ala (Glory be to Allah, and He is The High).

[2] pbuh: Peace Be Upon Him (The Prophet).

Special prayers and Du`a' go to the many teachers, scholars and `Ulamaa' who were directly tutoring this author at the time of his youth. Through the efforts of Shaikh Muhammad `Umar Da'ooq, the following is a partial list of the teachers who taught this author: Dr. Mustafa Siba`ee; Shaikh Muhammad M. Al-Sawwaf; Dr. Muhammad Al-Zo`by; Shaikh Muhammad `Itani; Shaikh Muhammad M. Da`ooq; Shaikh Al-Fudail Al-Wartalani; Shaikh Muhammad `Abdel Kareem Al-Khattabi; Shaikh Malik Bennabi; Shaikh Faheem Abu`Ubeyh; Shaikh Muhammad Al-Shaal; Dr. Sa`eed Ramadan; Atty. `Abdel Hakeem `Abideen; Dr. Tawfic Houri; Shaikh Abu Salih Itani; Shaikh Hashim Daftardar Al-Madani; and the late Shaikh Abdul Badee` Sakr. May Allah bless them and reward them.

A final prayer is to the readers who took the time to read this book. May Allah (swt) bless them all.

Allahumma Ameen.

SUPPLICATIONS

DU`A'

O Allah ! I seek refuge in You from anxiety and grief; I seek refuge in You from incapacity and laziness; and I seek refuge in You from the overcoming burden of debts and the overpowering of people.

O Allah ! I seek refuge in You from poverty except to You, from humiliation except for You, and from fear except from You.

O Allah ! I seek refuge in You from stating a false testimony, or committing immorality, or provoking You; and I seek refuge in You from the malice of the enemies, and from enigmatic disease, and from the despair of hope.

O Allah ! I seek refuge in You from the wicked people, from the worries of the livelihood, and from the ill-nature such as from bad attitude.

O Allah ! You are the Mercy of the mercies, and You are the Lord of the universe.

O Allah
Allahumma Ameen

اللَّهُمَّ

اللَّهُمَّ إِنِّي أَعُوذُ بِكَ مِنَ الْهَمِّ وَالْحَزَنِ
وَأَعُوذُ بِكَ مِنَ الْعَجْزِ وَالْكَسَلِ
وَأَعُوذُ بِكَ مِنْ غَلَبَةِ الدَّيْنِ وَقَهْرِ الرِّجَالِ
اللَّهُمَّ إِنِّي أَعُوذُ بِكَ مِنَ الْفَقْرِ إِلَّا إِلَيْكَ
وَمِنَ الذُّلِّ إِلَّا لَكَ وَمِنَ الْخَوْفِ إِلَّا مِنْكَ
وَأَعُوذُ بِكَ أَنْ أَقُولَ زُورًا أَوْ أَغْشَى فُجُورًا
أَوْ أَكُونَ بِكَ مَغْرُورًا وَأَعُوذُ بِكَ
مِنْ شَمَاتَةِ الْأَعْدَاءِ وَعُضَالِ الدَّاءِ
وَخَيْبَةِ الرَّجَاءِ اللَّهُمَّ إِنِّي أَعُوذُ بِكَ
مِنْ شَرِّ الْخَلْقِ وَهَمِّ الرِّزْقِ وَسُوءِ الْخُلُقِ
يَا أَرْحَمَ الرَّاحِمِينَ وَيَا رَبَّ الْعَالَمِينَ

I. INTRODUCTION

Islam is the youngest religion in the history of mankind, and Muslims do exceed 1.9 billion in number. While there is no coercion or compulsion in religion, there are no missionary activities either. However, Islam is the fastest growing religion in the world. At the same time, it is the only religion that has been misunderstood. The number of Muslims in North America exceeds ten million. At the same time, Muslims have been misunderstood, mistreated, mislabeled and abused.

Islam is the most tolerant religion and Muslims are also considered to be tolerant to the non-Muslims. However, there is a lack of communication and a lack of effective dialogue between Muslims and non-Muslims.

This humble effort is a step forward in the right direction in bringing people closer to one another. It is only through proper communication, and correct information that people will be able to understand one another better. It is also through education that people will be able to appreciate one another and their differences.

Ignorance and staying uninformed are causes of many problems among people of the world. One should be concerned enough to read more about others. Reading should be done through the writings of other groups about themselves. One should not read about others only from the writings of those outside the group about which they are writing. It should be from writers within their respective groups in order to get the correct information without bias or prejudice. In so doing, one will be more educated, knowledgeable, amicable, and tolerant towards others.

It should be mentioned here that if Almighty God (Allah) wished, he would have made everyone the same. It seems He wanted us to be different so that we would enjoy the beauty of life that He created for us. And it seems that He wanted us to approach Him with different methods. Therefore, it is not the method of approach to God that counts, but it is the intention, as long as the method is lawful, direct and decent.

In this booklet, the author has included: Terminologies, Sources of Islam, Islamic Principles, Practices of Islam, Other Aspects of stereotypes, Muslims in America, Contributions or Early Muslims, Contributions of Muslims in America, non-Muslims, Benefits of Becoming a Muslim, What Needs To Be Done, This is not Islam, living together, tolerance, and witness of non-Muslims, The situation, and Final Remarks.

It is the hope of the author that non-Muslims will appreciate what Islam and Muslims have to offer in order to build a better society of nations for the future.

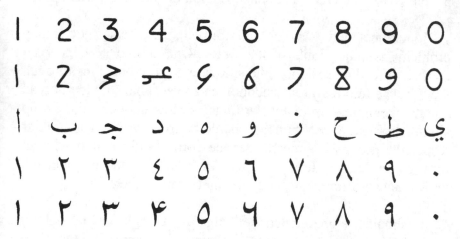

NUMERALS IN DIFFERENT SEMATIC LANGUAGE

II. TERMINOLOGIES

A. Islam and Muslims

Mohammedanism and Mohammadans are two misnomers for Islam and Muslims. If these terminologies were to be accepted, one might conclude that the religion of Islam has derived its name from a mortal person, Muhammad; and Islam becomes no more than another "ism" similar to Judaism, Hinduism, Marxism, Socialism, Arabism, Nationalism, etc. One might also think wrongly that Mohammedans are worshipers of Muhammad (pbuh) or believers in him in the same way as Christians believe in Jesus. One more misinterpretation would be that Muhammad (pbuh) was the founder of Islam. All these are wrong and misleading, and so these misnomers are rejected by Islam and its followers.

The true name of this religion is Islam, the root of which is Silm and Salaam, which means peace. Salaam may also mean greeting one another with peace. One of the beautiful names of God is that He is the Peace. It means more than that: Submission to One God, and to live in peace with the Creator, within one's self, with other people and with the environment. Thus, Islam is a total system of living.

The followers of Islam are called Muslims. A Muslim tries to live in peace and harmony with all these segments; hence, a Muslim is any person anywhere in the world whose obedience, allegiance, and loyalty are to God, the Lord of the Universe.

B. Muslims and Arabs

Muslims are not to be confused with Arabs. Muslims may be Arabs, Turks, Persians, Indians, Pakistanis, Malaysians,

Indonesians, Europeans, Africans, Americans, Hispanics, Chinese, Russians, or other nationalities. They constitute the rainbow of Islam, and they are united with the bond of brotherhood and submission to the One God, Allah (swt).

An Arab could be a Muslim, a Christian, a Jew, an agnostic, or an atheist. Any person who adopts the Arabic Language is called an Arab. However, the Language of the Qur'an (the Holy Book of Islam) is Arabic. Muslims all over the world try to learn Arabic so that they might be able to read the Qur'an and understand its meaning. They pray in the language of the Qur'an, namely Arabic. Supplications to God could be in any Language.

While there are 1.9 Billion Muslims in the world, there are about 400 million Arabs. Among them, approximately ten percent are not Muslim. Thus Arab Muslims constitute only about twenty percent of the Muslim population of the world.

C. Allah the Only One God

Allah (swt) is the name of the One and Only One God. Allah (swt) has ninety-nine beautiful Names, such as: The Gracious, The Merciful, The Beneficent, The Creator, The All-Knowing, The All-Wise, The Lord of the Universe, the First, the Last and others...

He is the Creator of human beings. He is the God for the Christians, the Jews, the Muslims, the Buddhists, the Hindus, the Atheists, and others. Muslims worship God whose proper name is Allah (swt). They put their trust in Him and they seek

His help and His guidance. He is neither male or female,, and we are not of His image.

D. Muhammad

Muhammad (pbuh) was chosen by God to deliver His Message of Peace, namely Islam. He was born in 570 CE (Common Era) in Makkah, Arabia. He was entrusted with the Message of Islam when he was at the age of forty years. The revelation that he received is called the Qur'an, while the Message is called Islam.

Muhammad is the very last prophet of God to mankind. He is the final Messenger of God. His Message was and still is to the Christians, the Jews, and the rest of Mankind. He was sent to those religious people to inform them about the true mission of Jesus, Moses, David, Jacob, Isaac, Abraham, Noah and many others. Muhammad (pbuh) is considered to be the summation, the purification and the culmination of all the prophets and messengers that came before him. He purified the previous messages from adulteration and completed the Message of God for all humanity. He was entrusted with the power of explaining, interpreting, and living the teachings of the Qur'an.

E. The Qur'an

The holy book of Islam is called the Qur'an. It was revealed unto Muhammad (pbuh) from Allah (swt) through Angel Gabriel (Jibril) for a period of 23 years. There is only one Qur'an in the whole world and it is in the Arabic Language. The Qur'an has one text, one language, and one dialects. It has been memorized by millions of Muslims in different parts of the world.

The Qur'an is composed of 114 Surah (chapters). It is to be read and recited with rules and regulations. When it is to be touched and when it is to be recited, a Muslim is to be in the state of cleanliness and purity (physical and spiritual). The authenticity and the totality of the Qur'an have been documented and recognized. The Qur'an cannot be translated and still be the Qur'an. It should have been mentioned here that it is the exact words of Allah (swt). Any translation is considered to be the explanation to the meaning of the Qur'an.

F. Hadith

The sayings and traditions of Prophet Muhammad (pbuh) are called the Hadith. These are real explanations, interpretation, and the living example of the Prophet (pbuh) for the teachings of the Qur'an. His sayings are found in books called Hadith books. The six famous collections of Hadith are Imam Al-Bukhari, Imam Muslim, Imam An-Nasa'i, Imam Abu Dawood, Imam At-Tarmizi, and Imam Ibn Majah.

G. Sunnah

In general, the word Sunnah means habit, practice, customary, procedure, or action, norm and usage sanctioned by tradition. Specification, any time the word Sunnah is mentioned, it is to refer to Prophet Muhammad (pbuh). Here it means his sayings, practices, and living habits. The Hadith of the Prophet (pbuh) is part of his Sunnah. The two major legal sources of jurisprudence in Islam are Qur'an and Sunnah. The

Sunnah is to confirm what is mentioned in the Qur'an. The Sunnah has a high authority in Islam; and Allah (swt) in many places in the Qur'an orders Muslims to follow the teachings of Prophet Muhammad (pbuh).

H. Sirah

The writings of the companions of the Prophet (pbuh) about him, his personality, his life history, and his ways of handling different situations are called Sirah. The famous collections of Sirah are At-Tabari, Ibn Ishaq, and Ibn Hisham. The Sirah is a source of reference that Muslims rely on in their daily life situations and problems.

I. Shari'ah

The Root of this word is Shara'a; and some other names of it are *Shar'*, *Shir'ah*, and *Tashri'*. The *Shari'ah* is the revealed and the Canonical laws of the religion of Islam. The legislator in Islam is only Allah (swt). It is He who has the right to legislate what is lawful (Halal) and what is prohibited (Haram) or unlawful. While the Legislative power in the government is in the hands of legislative assembly, their role is to make the rules within the scope and dimensions of the Qur'an and the Sunnah of the Prophet. These rules constitute the Shari'ah. Any legislation against the Shari'ah is nil and void. It is considered as a matter of unfaithfulness and ungratefulness to Allah. It is Shirk, i.e., associating themselves with the power of Allah. For those who do such activities and decisions are doomed in this world and hell is waiting for them on the Day of Judgement.

The legal sources of Islam are the Qur'an and the Hadith. For their jurisprudence, Muslims rely also on the Sirah of the Prophet (pbuh), the decisions made by the Rightly Guided Caliphs, and the general consensus of the early Muslim jurists. In so doing, they will be able to know more about what is lawful (Halal), unlawful (Haram), innovation (Bid'ah), suspected (Mashbooth), or distasteful (Makrooh).

If Muslims are confronted with a contemporary situation, which may be not found in any of the above sources, they will rely on Analogy. However, such type of decision making should be based on the spirit of Islamic teachings. The following is a summary of the sources of Islamic Shari'ah:

1. The Qur'an: The Holy Book of God to the worlds
2. The Hadith and Sunnah of the Prophet (pbuh)
3. The Sirah: Life history of the Prophet (pbuh)
4. Ijmaa': The Unanimous decisions of the early Muslims 'Ulamaa' (scholars)
5. Qiyaas: Analogy
6. Isstihsaan: To choose the better between two alternatives for good reasons.
7. Masslaha Mursalah or Mutlaqah: The judge is to make his decision for the benefit of the public.
8. 'Urf: Customs and habits if they are not against the teachings of Islam.
9. Isstisshaab: Agreeing to the situation as it was decided and agreed upon before.
10. Shar' Maa Qabl: Laws prescribed to people before Islam and also prescribed to Muslims as well.
11. Mazhab Al-Sahabah: Opinions of the Rightly Guided Companions (Khulafaa' Rashidoon) of the Prophet (pbuh).

III. ISLAMIC PRINCIPLES

A. Oneness of God

God is One and Only One. He is not two in one, or three in one. This means that Islam rejects the idea of trinity or such a unity of God which simplies more than one God in one. Muslims put their trust in God whose proper name is Allah (swt). Their Allegiance, Loyalty and Obedience are all to Allah (swt).

B. Oneness of Mankind

Muslims believe that people are created equal in front of the Law of God. There is no superiority for one race over another. God made us of different colors, nationalities, languages and beliefs so as to test who is going to be better than others. No one can claim that he is better than others. It is only God Who Knows who is better. It depends on piety, righteousness, and good intention.

C. Oneness of Messengers and the Message

Muslims believe that God sent different messengers throughout the history of mankind. All came with the same message and the same teachings. It was the people who misunderstood and misinterpreted them.

In Islam, there are five mighty prophets. They are: Noah, Abraham, Moses, Jesus and Muhammad (pbuh). The Prophets of Christianity and Judaism are indeed the Prophets of Islam.

D. Other Creatures

Muslims believe that there are unseen creatures in the universe created by God for special missions. Such creatures are Angles, Jinns, and others that are unknown yet to us.

Angles are made out of light while Jinns are made out of fire. Jibril (Archangel Gabriel) is an example of an angel, while Satan is an example of Jinn.

There are Creatures on the other planets as well; if Allah wishes, He would allow us to meet them in the future.   (42:29)

E. Day of Judgement

Muslims believe that there is a Day of Judgement where all people of the world throughout the history of mankind till the last day of life on earth, are to be brought for accounting, reward and punishment. The value and the duration of this life compared to the ever-lasting life in the hereafter is similar to this formula: X over infinity is zero: i.e., X over infinity approaches to zero. Similarly, the happiness of this life compared to the Bliss of Paradise reaches zero. On the other hand, the sorrows, calamities, torture, persecution, and/or punishment of this life compared with that of Hell reaches zero.

F. Innocence of Man at Birth

Muslims believe that all people are born free of sin. It is only after they reach the age of puberty and it is only after they commit sins that they are to be charged for their mistakes. No one is responsible for or can take the responsibility for the sins of others. However, the door of forgiveness through true repentance is always open.

G. Salvation

Islam teaches that people must work out their salvation through the guidance of God (Allah). This means that a person has to combine his belief and practice in his daily life activities. No one can act on behalf of someone else or even intercede between him and Allah (swt). Allah does not accept lip service from people.

To have true salvation, a person has to have belief in Allah (swt), good intentions, and good deeds in his life. With the Mercy and Blessings of Allah (swt), he will attain forgiveness and enter Paradise. To be forgiven for any single mistake, one has to make repentance to Allah directly without any confession to any person, or even without any intercession of anybody. Conditions for forgiveness are tied up with two situations. First, if someone made a mistake against any creature, he should apologize to the other person, before he requests the forgiveness of Allah. Second, if a mistake has been made against the teachings of Allah, the following items are to be considered before forgiveness is granted by Allah.

- One has to make a special prayer of Repentance (Tawba)
- He should admit privately and directly to Allah for his weakness in committing such a silly mistake
- He should promise Allah not to repeat the same mistake.

- He should promise Allah to take the initiative and do the good deeds preceded by the good intention.

Since Allah is the Most Gracious, Most Merciful and the forgiver; and since there is no original sin in Islam, Allah Almighty will give forgiveness to the ones who committed mistakes.

H. Freedom

This is a general term to mean several things at one time. Islam came to free people from slavery and to give them freedom to worship their Creator. There is no compulsion in religion. At the same time, Islam instructed that people are not to worship or follow any creature, any ideology, and/or system other than the Creator namely Allah (swt). They are to obey Him and to follow His teachings and instructions.

While freedom of religion was granted in Islam for the followers of any revealed divine religion, freedom of speech was also granted to all and to every person. The members of the Islamic communities are asked to speak their minds, to advise their leaders and to correct them if they make mistakes. Muslims are to speak the truth. Therefore, freedom of speech is in reality freedom of and for the Ultimate truth.

It should be mentioned here that One of the Beautiful Names of Allah (swt) is that He is the Truth. Hence, the Source of Truth has to come from Him, too. When a person is to speak he should know that he is accountable for whatever he says, as well as for his intention. He should remember that freedom of speech has its limitation and its sanctity. One's freedoms stop where another's begin for less than this would not be freedom, but injury. Whoever transgresses his limits should realize that he is responsible and accountable. A Muslim will not speak except the truth and only the truth. Lying is a big vice and Islam condemns liars as well as those who spread rumors or fabricate stories.

I. Equality of Genders

Men and woman are equal in the sight of God Almighty and the law of heaven. Both are complementary to one another, and both have the right to work together with respect and honor. The position of women in Islam is highly regarded, and even heaven is under the feet of the mothers. Children are instructed to respect their parents and to treat them with kindness and humbleness.

J. Position of Woman

The following are concepts concerning woman in Islam.

- Woman is a full and equal partner of man in the procreation of mankind
- She is equal to man in bearing personal and common responsibilities, and in receiving rewards for her deeds.
- She is equal to man in pursuit of education and knowledge.
- She is entitled to freedom of expression as much as man is.
- Women participated in public life with early Muslims.
- Islam grants woman equal rights to contracts, enterprise, and to earn and possess independently.

- Islam safeguarded these rights and put them in practice as integral articles of faith.
- Her inheritance and her earnings are hers; while her husband's inheritance and earnings are for the whole family.
- She enjoys more privileges than man:

  a. She is exempt from prayers/fasting in her menstrual cycle and at times of confinement.
  b. She is also exempt from attending the obligatory congregation of Friday prayers.
  c. She is exempt from all financial liabilities.
  d. As a mother, she enjoys recognition and higher honor in the sight of Allah (31:14-15); (16:15) and in the sight of the Prophet.

- Her rights and duties are equal to man but not necessarily identical with them.

K. State and Religion

Muslims believe that Islam is a total and complete way of life. It encompasses all aspects of life. As such, the teachings of Islam do not separate religion from politics. As a matter of fact, state and religion are under the obedience of Allah through the teachings of Islam. Hence, economic and social transactions, as well as educational and political systems are also part of the teachings of Islam.

L. Jihad

It is an Arabic word the root of which is Jahada, which means to strive for a better way of life. The nouns are Juhd, Mujahid, Jihad, and Ijtihad. The other meanings are endeavor, strain, exertion, effort, diligence, and fighting to defend one's life, land and religion.

Jihad should not be confused with Holy War; the latter does not exist in Islam nor will Islam allow its followers to be involved in a Holy War. The latter refers to the Holy War of the Crusaders against Muslims. Jihad is not a war to force the faith on others, as some people may think. It should never be interpreted as a way of compulsion of the belief on others, since there is an explicit verse in the Qur'an that says:

"There is no compulsion in religion." (2:256)

Jihad is not a defensive war only, but a war against any unjust regime. If such a regime exists, a war is to be waged against the leaders, but not against the people of that country. People should be freed from the unjust regimes and their influences so that they can freely choose to believe in Allah.

Not only in peace but also in war Islam prohibits terrorism, kidnapping, and hijacking, when carried against civilians. Whoever commits such violation is considered a murderer in Islam, and is to be punished by Islamic State. During wars, Islam prohibits Muslim soldiers from harming civilians, women, children, elderly, and the religious men like priests and rabbis. It also prohibits cutting down trees and destroying civilization constructions.

M. Holy War

In Islam there is nothing called Holy. The only Holy God is the Creator. His words are Holy. His revelations are Holy and His Teachings are also Holy. As far as war is concerned, there is nothing in the Qur'an or even in the teachings of Islam that Muslims should wage a war at all. Moreover, it is against the teachings of Islam to practice what is called Holy War. This action is not at all from Islam. It is a borrowed terminology from the Crusades.

Indeed the crusades of the Romans had used this terminology and applied it in action. They considered the local people in the M.E. as infidels. It happened that those people of the M.E. were Christian and Muslim Arabs. Even those Christians did not accept the Crusaders as their leaders. Hence, the Romans had to get the verdict and the blessings of the then the Pope to wage a tragic war against the M.E. people. They considered the local Christians and Muslims as Infidels.

In order to raise enough money to buy ammunition, they started selling croissant pastries in their local churches. They thought that croissant is the symbol for Muslims, i.e. crescent and star. This was not true of course. Muslims do not worship the moon. They worship Allah (swt) alone. Muslims do use both Lunar and solar calendars in their religious services. Their pledge of allegiance is only to Allah (swt), the Creator of the whole universe.

At that time the crusades killed 200,000 local people in the M.E. Similarly one can say that the Inquisition in Spain took place by the Francos against the local Muslims, Christians and

Jews. They killed 10 million Muslims and 4,000 Jews. These acts of terrorism were done in the name of their religion. However, Jesus was innocent of their terror, and Christianity and other Christians of the world are innocent of their crimes and atrocities.

N. Halal / Haram

These are two Arabic words to mean lawful and unlawful. The standards are based on the Qur'an and Hadith. Muslims are to abide in their daily life activities by the teachings of their standards.

These two concepts are very important when one talks about moral, physical, spiritual, medical, biological, and dietetic aspects of Islam. Muslims talk regularly about Halal and Haram for anything they do in life.

When Muslims talk about meat, for example, they use the terminology of *zabiha* to mean Halal; hence it will be lawful to be eaten.

O. Destiny

Many people misunderstood the concept of destiny and its implications in life. In Islam there is something called destiny and there is something called freedom of choice.

People did not have the choice to be born or not. They did not choose their parents and did not choose to come as male or female. They did not have the choice to be born in America, Europe, Africa, Asia or Australia. At the same time they did not have a choice to as where, when and how to die. All of the above decisions are destined to us and they are in the Hands of Allah (swt). Accordingly, Allah will never ask us about these decisions that He made for us. They are His responsibilities. Moreover, if a person dies before the age of puberty, he/she will go automatically to heaven.

After the age of puberty we are all responsible for our deeds and actions as well as for our thoughts and intentions. We are also responsible for our planning and manipulations. If and when we do good and are having good intentions, we are to be rewarded. The reward is given ten times for every good act.

For those who never heard about Allah, and the Message that He gave to His Prophet Muhammad (pbuh), they will be charged according to their mentality and their action preceded by their intentions. Allah has ninety-nine Beautiful Names. One of these is that He is the Just (Al-Adil). He will treat each one with fairness and ultimate justice.

Blessed be the name of your Lord,
full of Majesty, Bounty and Honor.
[Qur'an, 55:78]

18

IV. PRACTICES OF ISLAM

God instructed the Muslims to practice what they believe. In Islam, there are five pillars, namely:

A. Declaration of Creed (Shahada)

The verbal commitment and pledge that there is only One God and that Muhammad (pbuh) is the Messenger of God, is considered to be the Creed of Islam. This means that a Muslim puts his trust in God, the Almighty. His loyalty, his allegiance and his obedience are all to the Creator, Allah (swt). If and when there is a conflict of interest between his desires and God, he will deny himself in favor of obeying Allah (swt).

It is understood that Prophet Muhammad (pbuh) was the one who had the privilege to explain, interpret and live the teachings of the Qur'an. Hence, a Muslim is to listen, obey and follow the teachings of the Prophet, too, so that he will earn the blessings of Allah (swt), the Creator.

B. Prayer (Salat)

The Performance of five daily prayers is required by Islam. These prayers have to be performed at specific times during the day and the night. These five obligatory prayers are: Fajr (Dawn), Zuhr (Noon), 'Asr (Afternoon), Maghrib (Sunset), and Isha' (Late Night). Each prayer is called Salat.

The Friday Congregational Prayer (Jumu'ah) is also a must for Muslim men but optional for Muslim Women. It is to be performed in the Mosque. It can also be performed in any convenient place when there is no Mosque in the area.

There are many optional prayers that Muslims perform along with those obligatory prayers. Some special prayers also exist, as praying before burying a dead Muslim, praying before travelling, praying on the 'Eid Days, and praying to get guidance when one cannot decide between two choices. A Muslim may pray anywhere in the world whether he/she is in a Mosque, a house, an office, or outside. The whole world is a place of worship. However, the reward is much greater when the prayers are performed in-groups. Congregational prayers (Jamaa'ah) in the Mosques are strongly recommended for Muslims.

C. Fasting (Sawm)

Fasting is a total abstinence of food and liquids from dawn to sunset during the entire month of Ramadan. Married Muslims also have to refrain from intimate relationship from dawn to sunset during that period. Muslims can still enjoy all these things during the nighttime of Ramadan from sunset till dawn. They usually eat a meal right after sunset called Iftar, which means breakfast, and another light meal right before dawn called Sahur. The purpose of fasting is to acquire the concept of Taqwa. The latter might be defined as self-control, self-restraint, self-discipline, self-obedience, self-training, self-consciousness, self-education, and self-evaluation. Fasting does help the person to improve himself physically, biologically, mentally, psychologically, and spiritually.

D. Purifying Tax (Zakat)

This is an annual payment of certain percentage of a Muslim's property, which is distributed among the poor or other rightful beneficiaries in the society. These categories are: the poor, the needy, the sympathizers, the captives, the debtors, and the wayfarers, for those who are to collect it and to administrate it, and for the cause of Allah (swt). The amount to be collected is 2.5%, 5%, or 10%, depending on the type of assets and the method used to produce the wealth.

E. Pilgrimage (Hajj)

The performance of pilgrimage to Makkah is required once in a lifetime, if means available. Hajj is in part for memory of the trials and tribulations for Prophet Abraham, his wife Hagar, and his only son Prophet Ismail. It is considered the fifth pillar of Islam. Hajj is to be performed in the first ten days of the last month every lunar calendar, called Zul-Hijjah. There are rules and regulations and specific dress to be followed. The benefits of Hajj are too many to be counted. It has spiritual beliefs, as well as social, cultural, economic and political advantages. (For more information, you can read our book: Hajj and Umrah)

The above mentioned items are the main pillars of Islam for any human being who wishes to become a Muslim. For a practicing Muslim, he usually tries his best to practice not only the pillars, but also the rest of the teachings of Islam. These include the religious, the social, the cultural, the educational, the economic, the political, and the moral aspects of Islam. While a Muslim is fulfilling these teachings, his intention is to obey the Creator, namely God Almighty.

V. OTHER RELATED ASPECTS

A. Calendar

Islamic practices are based on the Lunar Calendar. However, Muslims also use the Gregorian Calendar in their daily religious lives. Hence, the Islamic calendar includes both the Common Era and the time of migration (Hijra) of the Prophet of Islam from Makkah to Madinah in the year of 623 CE.

The Islamic calendar is 11 or 12 days shorter than the Gregorian calendar. The names of the Islamic months are: Muharram, Safar, Rabie Awwal, Rabie Thani, Jamadi Awwal, Jamadi Thani, Rajab, Sha'ban, Ramadhan, Shawwal, Zul Qi'da, and Zul Hijjah.

B. Celebrations (Eids)

Muslims have two celebrations (Eids); namely, Feast of Sacrifice (Eidul Adha) and Feast of Fast-Breaking (Eidul Fitr). The Eid of Sacrifice is in remembrance of the sacrifice to be by Prophet Abraham of his son Ismail. The Eid of Fast-Breaking comes at the end of the month of fasting, Ramadhan.

C. Diets

Islam allows Muslims to eat everything, which is good for the health. It restricts certain items such as pork and is by-products, alcohol, and any narcotic or addictive drugs. Among the prohibited food is meat of animals that are strangled, beaten to death, killed by a fall, killed by being smitten with the horn, and which other beasts have been eaten, except those that have been slaughtered in the proper manner.

Prevention is better than treatment of a disease, and dieting is the safest way to better health. It is good to mention here that the personality, character, behavior, and overall performance of the individual, are affected by the food eaten, and therefore, one has to select the best type of food for his good health.

There is thus a linkage between physical and mental heath. A proverb related to this subject has been narrated by saying: "A sound mind is in a sound body."

D. Place of Worship

The place of Worship is called Mosque or Masjid. There are three holy places of worship for Muslims in the world, These are Mosque of Ka'bah in Makkah, Mosque of Prophet Muhammad in Madina, and Masjid Al-Aqsa, adjacent to Dome of the Rock in Jerusalem, Palestine.

A Muslims may pray anywhere in the world whether in a Mosque, a house, an office, or outside. The whole world is a place of worship. It is preferable that Muslims pray in a congregation; however, he/she may pray individually anywhere. Muslims come to the House of Allah to pray and to ask forgiveness. They are to learn their religion and they are to try to apply its teachings in their private and public life. They come to the Masjid to earn blessings, mercy and guidance from Allah. As a conclusion, Muslims are to obey Allah and to follow His rules and regulations as much as possible, especially in the House of worship.

E. Holiday

The holy day of the Muslims is Friday. It is considered to be sacred and the Day of Judgement will take place on Friday. Muslims join together shortly after noon on Friday for the Friday congregational prayer in a Mosque. A leader (Imam) gives a sermon (Khutbah) and leads the congregational prayer.

F. Festivities

In Islam, there are a few festivities that Muslims enjoy. Some of them are Islamic traditions (Sunnah), while others are habits and customs. Some of the festivities are the following:
1. Festivity of Marriage
2. Festivity of Wedding (Waleemah)
3. Harvest Festivity (Al- Hisad)
4. Circumcision Festivity (Al-Khitan)
5. Bismillah party refers to the time when a child starts reading Qur'an.
6. Ameen party refers to the time when a child finishes reading the whole Qur'an.
7. Prophet's Birthday. Prophet Muhammad (pbuh) did not celebrate his own birthday, and he did not instruct any of his companion's ® to celebrate his birthday. None of them celebrated their own birthdays as they believed it would be an innovation (Bid'ah). However, very many Muslims in different parts of the world do celebrate the birthday of the Prophet, or they do commemorate his life history (Sirah).

G. Family Life:

The cornerstone of a society is a good family. Islam encourages people to get married and have a stable family. The latter is based on rights and responsibilities on both husband and the wife. Islam recognizes the social necessity, the religious virtues and the moral aspect of marriages. There is no premarital relation as much as there is no extramarital relationship. Homosexuality and incest are condemned in Islam.

Family in Islam is composed of: Parents, children, grand-parents, grandchildren, uncles, aunts, nephews and nieces from both sides of husband and wife. When a young couple marries each other they are to integrate their extended families to unite as one. They become an integral part of the big family in the society. There are rules and regulations of a stable family. There are obligations and duties in as much as there are rights and privileges.

Since the structure of a family is very important to the individual, to the family, to the social and to the government, the following are partial concepts and foundations that Islam laid:

- The family is the cornerstone and the foundation of a social, cultural and religious structure in a society.
- God created people from a single soul and made the spouse a mate from him.

- Then God created from the same soul, men and women in large numbers. Therefore, we should fear, respect, and appreciate Allah for His creation.

- From among His signs are mates (spouses), who have been created, so that they may dwell in tranquility. To fulfill this objective, He has made compassion, love, sympathy, concern and mercy between the two spouses.

- Allah has made all of the above so that we may think, ponder, contemplate and reflect.

- The marriage life is a matter of worship, just like those of praying, fasting, and other religious acts. Hence, it is considered to be a fulfillment of the faith of the individuals.

- Love between the couple starts after marriage. If love starts before marriage, it will stop after marriage or else it will be diminished and diluted.

- During the process of courtship (Khitbah), and before performing the marriage ceremony (Nikah), the two individuals should know one another. However, there should be no privacy between them. The members of the two families are to be included also.

- For an official marriage to take place, an officiation has to be performed, and there should be witnesses, preferable from their blood relatives.

- The concept of "mahr" or dowry is to be offered by the groom to the bride. It is a token commitment of the groom to the bride that he is to be responsible for the family financially.

- For marriage to take place, one should look for the girl who is compassionate, pious, tender and bashful. There are some individuals who marry girls for fame, reputation, money, and beauty or even for obtaining the

Green Card or residency of U.S.A. All these are false hopes, desires and worldly lusts. If any of these items come along with the girl as a secondary benefit, they are well and good. One should not put them as priorities.

- After marriage ceremony takes place, or after the marriage has been consummated, it is recommended that a "Waleemah" is to be offered. It is a matter of a dinner where relatives and friends are invited.

- It is recommended that Khitbah (courtship) and Nikah (Marriage) ceremonies and the Waleemah are to be publicized. The marriage union of the couple is not to be publicized.

- Marriage is for worldly and heavenly benefits, both at the same time.

- Marriage helps a person to live a stable life – morally, socially, psychologically, culturally, spiritually, economically, biologically, etc…

Allah is the Light of the Heavens and the Earth   (Qur'an 24.35)

VI. STEREOTYPES

A. General

In America, there are many stereotypes and accusations against Islam and Muslims. This type of abuse could be due to lack of communication, misinformation, or an outlet for the frustration of the non-Muslims from their own societies and its problems.

While doing research, one may be able to find out that there have been many more stereotypes against the other national, ethnic, and religious groups. Some of these groups are: the American Indians, the Blacks, the Catholics, the Jews, the Italians, the Greeks, the Polish, the Japanese, the Chinese, the Koreans, the Vietnamese, the Hispanics, including Puerto Ricans, and most recently, are the Arabs and Muslims.

B. Causes

As far as Muslims and Arabs are concerned, one has to look deeply into the history and find out more reasons for this sad situation. When the crusaders invaded the Middle East, and when the Spanish Inquisition took place, many misconceptions were created against Islam and Muslims. A series of stereotypes were fabricated and spread. They were changed according to time, place and conditions, but the accusation is still prevailing. Muslims are put on the defensive side.

C. Old Stereotypes

Some of the old stereotypes and misinformation are: Muhammadanism for Islam, Mohammadans for Muslims, Arabs for Muslims, Black Muslims for Muslims, sexy, harem, slavery, camel Arab, killing non-Muslims to go to paradise, spreading Islam with the sword, Jihad, Holy war, polygamy, worshipping a black stone, Allah (swt) is a statue worshipped by Muslims, discrimination against women, etc... Such stereotypes and false information against Islam and Muslims created hatred, animosity, and a state of cold war against Muslims. Hence, Muslims were put on the defense and were made to be apologetic instead of being positive.

D. New Stereotypes

A new wave of stereotypes has spread recently against Islam and Muslims. Some of these are: fundamentalism, terrorism, hostage taking, hijacking, radicals, reactionaries, militancy, religious fanaticism, dictatorship, totalitarianism, monarchy, socialism, Arabism, nationalism, etc... All these and many more created an atmosphere of fear in the minds, hearts and souls of many innocent people all over the world. A few incidents have been polarized, dramatized, sensationalized and publicized beyond limits. These led to a state of animosity against Muslims and Arabs everywhere in the world.

E. Reform

It is incumbent that these stereotypes and accusations need to be cleared away and cleaned up; otherwise, it will be impossible to create peace, understanding, and harmony between Muslims and non-Muslims. In order to do that, one has to realize that Islam is not to be blamed because of a few incidents committed by some individual Muslims. At the same time, Christianity and Judaism are not to be blamed because of what some of the Christians and the Jews are doing wrong. Also Muslims, Christians and Jews of the world are not to be blamed for whatever is done wrong by some members of their particular faiths. Americans are not to be blamed for anything that goes wrong in the White House, in the state Department, or even in the CIA.

I bear witness that there is no deity except Allah and I bear witness that Muhammad is the Messenger of Allah

VII. CONTRIBUTIONS OF EARLY MUSLIMS

The early Muslims were highly educated. They contributed to modern civilization through many fields. Their major cities of enlightenment were Makkah, Madinah, Cordova, Al-Hamra, Toledo, Timbuktu, Cairo, Damascus, Baghdad, Fez, Tunisia City, etc.

Some contributions were in the field of:

1. Language: 10,000 words in Arabic are found in the English language.
2. Arithmetic: the present English numbers and the zero are the inventions of early Muslims.
3. Algebra, logarithm and calculus.
4. Chemistry, Physics, and Medicine.
5. Geography and navigation
6. Astronomy and the calendar using solar and lunar systems at the same time.
7. Ibn Khaldoun's economic theory is that inflation can be lowered by making more jobs available in the country. Mr. Reagan, former president of the U.S.A., quoted Ibn Khaldoun in one of his speeches in 1982.
8. Banking without interest: Islam preached the concept of sharing in the capital and in the profit rather than having a very small benefit called interest.
9. Islam eliminated the economic exploitation of the poor by the rich in a capitalistic system.
10. Islam has also eliminated dictatorship, monarchy, totalitarian systems or feudal systems.

Islamic scholars learned Greek sciences. They translated them into Arabic and augmented their thoughts with fresh ideas. The substance of which outshines even today's scientific and philosophical advancement. Muslim learned men were motivated and driven by an internal spiritual force and, as a consequence, their contributions were qualitative. Alhazen did not conceive of light in the same way as modern Western scientists regard it. To him, light was a source of internal illumination of heart and mind. Nevertheless, he determined its behavior, studied its nature, and postulated its physical concreteness; yet it remained a source of illumination and as a gift of Allah (swt) to man - His best creation.

1. On the other hand, Western scientists approach science and technology from a quantitative and materialistic point of view. To Kepler and Newton, physical concreteness remains the only objective and thus a focal point of utility. Within their souls, there remained a sense of emptiness. Muslim scholars set out, invariably, to serve the cause of Allah (swt).

2. As the land of Islam expanded, so did the number of believers who wanted to perform the duty of Hajj. Hence there was a need for travel, direction, and the necessities of life. Maps were prepared, extensive travels were undertaken, geology and geography of iterim lands studied, including the religions of non-Muslims. Devices and instruments were invented to facilitate the carrying out of the Islamic obligation of prayer, and the correct direction of the Holy Ka'bah.

3. No group of people ever loved their leader as much as Muslims loved their Prophet (May the peace and blessings of Allah (swt) be on him); so to preserve his sayings, doings and orders, carefully documented and

extensive biographies were written. Thus, a new art of Historiography was developed. The Qur'an asks man to think about creation around him, so Muslim thinkers took upon themselves the study of Cosmology and Astronomy. Thus, Muslim science had at its center the teachings of Islam, which were the driving forces in the minds of Muslim intellectuals.

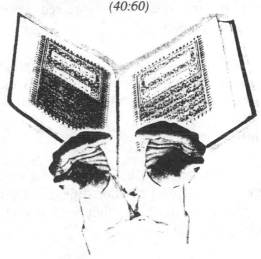

وَقَالَ رَبُّكُمُ ٱدْعُونِيٓ أَسْتَجِبْ لَكُمْ

"And our Lord says.: Call on me:
I will answer your prayer...."
(40:60)

« الدُّعَاءُ مُخُّ العِبَادَة »

"Supplication is the brain of worship."

VIII. MUSLIMS IN NORTH AMERICA

A. Classification

When we talk about America, we mean North America, i.e., U.S.A and Canada. Muslims in America may be classified according to the following groups: American Indians, Afro-American Muslims, and early Muslim immigrants from USSR, Turkey, Lebanon, Syria, Palestine, Albania, and Yugoslavia (Bosnia).

A late wave of immigrants came to America from India, Burma, Pakistan, Bangladesh, Afghanistan, Iran, Egypt, Sudan, Libya, Tunisia, Morocco, and the West Indies.

There is a group of students who came from the Muslim world to study in America. Their number exceeds half a million people. The other group are the reverts or returnees. These are the ones who accepted Islam from among the Americans themselves.

Finally, there is a small group of diplomats who try to serve their nationals in America. Sometimes they help Muslims in general for religious, cultural and educational purposes.

B. Number

The number of Muslims in America exceeds 10 million. They are of all nationalities, languages, and ethnic backgrounds. However, they are bound together with the teachings of Islam.

C. Distribution

The Muslims of America are distributed among the major and minor cities as well as university campuses. Some of the major cities are Washington, D.C., Boston, New York City, Jersey City, Newark, Cleveland, Buffalo, Detroit, Toledo, Dearborn, Chicago, Milwaukee, Michigan city, Indianapolis, Columbus, Cincinnati, Houston, Miami, Orlando, St. Louis, Cedar Rapids, St. Paul, Sacramento, San Francisco, San Jose, Los Angeles, San Diego, Phoenix, Tucson, Denver, Seattle, Anchorage, etc...

In Canada, they are distributed in Halifax, Montreal, Quebec, Ottawa, Kingston, Toronto, Hamilton, Mississuaga, Sudbury, London, Windsor, Winnipeg, Saskatchewan, Edmonton, Calgary, Lac La Biche, Fort MacMurry, Vancouver, etc...

D. Characteristics

Muslims of America, as a representative group, can be recognized by the following characteristics:

1. They are highly educated in every field of science, education and technology
2. They are family-oriented: the rate of divorce is minimal.
3. They are a peaceful community: the rate of crimes and juvenile delinquency is also minimum compared to any other ethnic or religious groups in America.

4. They are religiously oriented and committed, but they are not to be labeled as fanatics, radicals or fundamentalists.

5. They are conscientious about their dietary regulations as to what is permissible to eat and drink and what is prohibited for consumption.

6. They are health oriented with the concept of prevention through fasting and selective dieting. They are against the use of drugs or alcohol, as these are prohibited in Islam.

7. They are morally oriented and committed. Sex before marriage, extramarital relationships, and homosexuality are not permitted for Muslims, and are great sins.

8. The elderly are greatly respected and honored in a Muslim society.

9. They are hospitable and generous to their guests, and they enjoy having guests in their own houses.

10. They are friendly and are respectful to the non-Muslims. They do not believe in isolating themselves in ghettos, but to integrate and to exist within the society without losing their identity.

11. Concerning race, they are color-blind and they constitute the rainbow of Islam.

D. Contemporary Situation

After the Gulf War, and after the demolition of the Soviet Union as a superpower, the whole attention was directed against Islam and Muslims. Special attention was directed against the Muslims of U.S.A. A special report by a committee was from the congress have accused the Muslims of America by indicating that most of the Islamic Mosques are hubs of international terrorism. The paper of the committee was circulated in February 1993.

Mr. Muhammad Salah and Muhammad Jarad (both live in Chicago) were accused and put in Israeli jails. They were charged with helping HAMAS of Palestine while they were visiting their relatives in Palestine. It was found later that they were innocent.

Sheikh Umar Abdel Rahman, a blind Imam from Egypt and a Da'iya was accused of cheating the immigration Dept. Later he was charged as being a source of fundamentalism in U.S.A. Finally, he was charged as a source of motivating certain individuals to bomb the World Trade Center in New York. The author of this book passed a statement that was distributed during the turmoil. The press release goes as follows:

<u>Press Release (World Trade Center)</u>

We, the Muslims of America, condemn all types of atrocities, including terrorism, extremism, and killing of innocent people in different parts of the world. The attack on the World Trade Center of New York City is an outrageous crime. Whoever has done such an act is directly responsible and should be penalized accordingly.

Islam is the religion of Silm and Salaam. Silm and Salaam mean peace, tranquility, concord, and justice for all. Killing one person is like killing the whole mankind, as the Qur'an states in Chapter 5, Verse 32. Muslims are ordained to protect the lives of all human beings irrespective of their color, race, nationality, religion, creed, gender, or social status. However, it should be stated here that Islam, Judaism, and Christianity should not be blamed for any criminal act. Also, Muslims, Jews, and Christians are not to be accused or blamed for crimes committed by any individual. Criminals are responsible for their own personal crimes.

We the ten (10) million Muslims of America are living peacefully in our houses, jobs, mosques, and neighborhoods. We never entangled ourselves with any problem created in any Muslim country, although we are concerned as Muslims and as American citizens for the welfare of all. Muslims and non-Muslims alike. We are for justice to all.

We, therefore, demand from the authorities of the American government, not to associate the American Muslims with any individual act here or abroad. Similarly, we demand from the leaders of the mass media (TV, radio, print) not to intimidate the Muslims who are living peacefully as citizens of this loving country. Muslims of America have already demonstrated their loyalty and allegiance to America whether they are immigrants or native born. They also contributed to the success of the American dreams in most of the fields of science, technology, safe community, education, social structure, family values and other values.

We will continue to work hand-in-hand with all the Americans to improve the image of America, Islam, Christianity, Judaism, and other varieties of religions.

IX. CONTRIBUTIONS OF AMERICAN MUSLIMS

1. Sears Tower and the John Hancock Building in Chicago were designed by a Muslim chief architect who had migrated to the U.S. from the then East Pakistan (now Bangladesh).

2. Science and technology: Muslims in America are generally highly educated, and are involved in every field of education, science, and technology.

3. Foreign students at universities and colleges are great assets to the economic stability of academic institutions and to the local American societies and communities.

4. They comprise a melting pot of all nationalities of Muslims into the Ummah of Islam in America. The rainbow of Islam is demonstrated in their various hues and shades of color. The concept of multi-culturalism is also unique in them in theory and in practice.

5. Peace in society: they are one of the most peaceful communities is America. The rate of divorce among Muslims is minimal; the rate of juvenile delinquency is minimal; and the rate of crimes is also minimal.

6. Justice and equality to all, irrespective of color, nationality, creed, ethnic background, or social status, is demonstrated by Muslims.

7. Centers, mosques, and schools have been established by the Muslims without the help of the American government. A good amount of the money came from the Muslim world. America is the recipient and beneficiary of the wealth and brains of the Muslim world.

X. NON-MUSLIMS

This section is designed for non-Muslims so they realize their status in the Qur'an and in the history of the Muslim people. In so doing, non-Muslims may appreciate their positions in Islam more clearly. Hence, a better understanding may be created between Muslims and non-Muslims.

A. Non-Muslims in the Qur'an

1. According to the Qur'an, non-Muslims are those who do not believe in Allah and His last and final Messenger to mankind whose name is Muhammad. Non-Muslims may include any and all of the following groups of people:

   a. People of the Book (Christians, Catholics and Jews)
   b. Idol worshippers
   c. Agnostics
   d. Atheists
   e. Buddhists, Hindus and many others

According to the Qur'an, People of the Book have earned a good attention and a good status because their prophets received revelations from God. Some of their messengers were considered among the Mighty Prophets, especially Abraham, Moses and Jesus.

Muslims believe in all the Prophets of Allah to mankind, including Noah, Abraham, Isaac, Jacob, Ishmael, David, Solomon, Moses, Jesus and Muhammad. Muslims believe in the original revelations of God to those prophets, namely the Torah (first five books of the Old Testament), Zabur (Psalms of David), Injil (The New Testament) and Qur'an.

40

Muslims believe that the true religion of Christianity is found in the Qur'an, and that the true religion of Judaism is also found in the Qur'an. Muslims do honor, respect and admire these prophets and messengers. Islam commanded Muslims to honor, respect and protect the People of the Book. The message in the Qur'an teaches Muslims that God sent Prophet Muhammad to purify, correct, and complete the previous messages that came before Him.

2. People of the Book

As far as Christians are concerned, the following points are to be mentioned:

a. Muslims believe that Christians of all denominations and Sects are part of the People of the Book.

b. Many Christians are praised in the Qur'an several time. In Surah (chapter) "Al-Imran" (The Family of Imran), Allah (swt) informs us the following:

c. *"...Of the People of the Book there is a staunch community who recite the revelations of Allah in the night season, falling prostrate (before Him). They believe in Allah and the Last Day, and enjoin right conduct and forbid indecency, and vie one with another in good works. They are of the righteous. And whatever good they do, they will not be denied the need thereof. Allah is aware of those who ward off (evil)."* (3:113-114)

d. Muslims are told that Christians are nearest to the Muslims in affection, as they have priests, monks and preachers, and because they are inclined to be more humble than others. They are more inclined to listen to the revelations and recitation of the Qur'an. In Surah "Al-Imran", Allah says the following about the followers of Jesus:

"And lo! Of the People of the Scripture, there are some who believe in Allah and that which is revealed unto you and that which was revealed unto them, humbling themselves before Allah. They purchase not a trifling gain at the price of the revelations of Allah. Verily their reward is with their Lord, and lo! Allah is swift to take account." (3:199)

e. Muslims are informed in the Qur'an in Surah "Al-Maidah" (The Table Spread) that Allah (swt) praised those Christians who devote their time to Him in prayers.

The following is said about them:

"...And you will find the nearest of them in affection to those who believe (to be) those who say: Lo! We are Christians. That is because there are among them priests and monks, and because they are not proud. Then they listen to that which hath been revealed unto the messenger, you see their eyes overflow with tears because of their recognition of the Truth. They say: Our Lord, we believe. Inscribe us as among the witnesses." (5:82-83)

B. Non-Muslims in History

Christians and Jews have lived peacefully with Muslims for over fourteen centuries in the Middle East and in other Asian and African countries. Christians were welcomed by Prophet Muhammad (pbuh) in Madinah and a treaty of peace was signed inside his Masjid. The second Caliph, 'Umar, did not pray in the Church in Jerusalem so as not to give the Muslims an excuse to take it over. Christians trusted the Muslims, and so the key of the Church in Jerusalem is still in the hands of the Muslims. Jews fled from Spain during the Inquisition, and were welcomed by the Muslims. They settled in the heart of the Islamic Caliphate. They enjoyed positions in the Islamic Sate. Crusaders invaded the Middle East and occupied it for about 200 years. This occupation was accompanied with torture and persecution upon the local people. However, when Salahuddin liberated the land, he treated the Christians with respect, and he allowed the Jews to come and live with them.

Throughout the Muslim world, churches, synagogues, and missionary schools were built within the Muslim neighborhoods. Such places were protected by the Muslims even during the contemporary crises in the Muslim world. Non-Muslims have flourished in the Muslim world. The mere existence of their presence in large numbers in the Muslim world today proves the justice and tolerance of Islam and Muslims. Tolerance, justice, and co-existence are among the main teachings of Islam that lead to mutual understanding and a better way of life among all people. Islam does not allow Muslims to impose their beliefs on others. The Qur'an states that "there is no compulsion in religion." (2:256)

To this effect, Thomas Arnold said in his book The Call to Islam, the following:

"We have never heard about any attempt to compel non-Muslim parties to adopt Islam, or about any organized persecution aiming at exterminating Christianity. If the Caliphs had chosen one of these plans, they would have wiped out Christianity as easily as what happened to Islam during the reign of Ferdinand and Isabella in Spain, by the same method which Louis XIV followed to make Protestantism a creed whose followers were to be sentenced to death, or with the same ease of keeping the Jews away from Britain for a period of 350 years."

In his book, the Islamic Civilization, Mr. Adam Metzifi said the following:

The existence of the Christians among the Muslims was the reason for the appearance of the principle of tolerance for which the new reformers called. There was a need for co-existence and harmony that should prevail in all countries. This caused from the very beginning a kind of tolerance which was not known in Europe in the Middle Ages. The result of that tolerance was the birth of the Science of Comparative Religion."

"...And help one another in furthering virtue and God consciousness, and do not help one another in furthering evil and enmity..."
[Qur'an, 5:2]

X. THIS IS NOT ISLAM

While Islam is a total way of life and a complete system, which deals with the individual, the family, the community, government and international relations, it has been misunderstood because of situations prevailing in its homelands. While people write about Islam and what it stands for, there are many things that prevail in the Muslims world that are not from Islam. For the sake of clarity, those things that may exist in the Muslim world are not from Islam are mentioned. They may be anti-Islamic teachings or practices discouraged by Islam. This chapter presents what Islam does NOT stand for and what Islam is NOT about. Through the process of negation one may come closer to Islam and its teachings. Then, one may realize what Islam stands for. The following is a summary of those things that are NOT from Islam:

- Islam is not a religion in western sense although religious obligations are part of Islam. Islam is both a state and a religion at one time because it is a complete way of life, a total code of ethics, and a total system to be followed.

- Islam is NOT called Mohammedanism and the followers of Islam are not called Mohammedans. The word Islam is an Arabic word, the root of which is *silm* and *salaam*. These terms mean peace, greetings, and obedience to God (Allah). Whoever wishes to live in peace and harmony within himself, with his family, with society and, above all, with his Lord Allah is called a Muslim. Therefore, Muslims do NOT worship Muhammad and he is NOT the founder of Islam. The founder is Allah Himself. Muhammad is NOT a divine person and is NOT immortal. Hence, the followers of Islam are called Muslims and NOT Mohammedans. Their religion is called Islam and NOT Mohammedanism.

- The word Muslim is NOT a synonym for an Arab. Any person who speaks, communicates, reads and understand the Arabic language is an Arab. Therefore, to be an Arab is NOT a genetic and religious identity, but a person speaking the Arabic language. It was reported that the Prophet Muhammad said,

Arabic is the language of the tongue.

Hence, one may find Arab Christians, Arab Jews, Arab Muslims, and Arab agnostics. There are 1.9 Billion Muslims in the world among which is 400 million Arabs.

- Islam is NOT theocracy. There is no one person or particular group who represents God exclusively on earth. There is no Pope in Islam, and no one has the right to change or amend Islam to suit the conditions of a particular society. No one has the right to legislate rules and regulations be they religious, political, social or economic that are contrary to Islam. No one has even the right to interpret Islam according to his own wish or his own use. Islam has been explained, interpreted and lived as an exemplified life by the Messenger of Allah, Prophet Muhammad (peace be upon him).

- Islam is NOT a theology or theosophy. Islam is a total way of life dealing with social, educational, economical, political and religious practices. In Islam Allah is One and He is the only One to be worshipped. Of course, Islamic laws are from Allah, the Most High, and the Most Glorified.

- The Qur'an, the Holy Book of Muslims, is NOT a scripture. It is the Direct Word of Allah revealed to Prophet Muhammad (pbuh) through Angel Jibril (Gabriel). The Qur'an is the prime source of legislation for Muslims. The Hadith is the sayings of the Prophet Muhammad. The Sunnah is the tradition, the explanation, the interpretation and the living example of the Prophet himself. It is the second source of legislation for Muslims. The Seerah is the writings of the disciples of the Prophet about him (The Prophet) by the inspiration of Allah. This is the third source of Islamic law.

- There is NO priesthood or nunhood in Islam. A Muslim is to live and enjoy life as a human being. People on earth are human beings. They are not angels and they are not animals. They are expected to perform their duties and responsibilities as human beings within the framework of Islam.

- There is NO original sin and there is no concept of such sin. There is also NO confession in Islam.

- There is NO religious hierarchy in Islam, which is called Mullah, or Moulvi. The concept of Waliy as a wise man or as a saint is not from Islam. Whosoever goes to a Waliy or to the grave of a Waliy and asks anything is committing a sin against the teachings of Islam, and the acts is equivalent to polytheism or SHIRK.

- There is NO divinity in Islam attributable to any human being. Every person is a human being and cannot be elevated to the degree of being exalted to be divine.

- There is NO Sufism in Islam. Islam is Islam and Sufism is NOT Islam. A Muslim is a Muslim and a sufi person is a sufi, and twain do not meet. Allah selected the word Muslim as the name for all those who accepted the teachings of Islam directly from the Qur'an and Sunnah. There cannot be a prefix or a suffix for any Muslim.

- There are no sects in Islam. Islam cannot accept its followers being called Shi'ah or Sunni. Muhammad (pbuh) himself was neither one of these two groups. The Caliphs themselves were not. Imam Ali and his beloved two children Hassan and Hussain were neither Shi'ah nor Sunni. They were only Muslims. They were all the followers of the Prophet Muhammad himself.

- In Islam, there is NO monarchy. Islam never tolerated the existence of a monarchy in its homeland. Since there are monarchs presently in the Muslim world and in the heart of Islam, one has to realize that their presence is against the teachings of Islam. Monarchies do still exist in Saudi Arabia, Jordan, Kuwait, UAE, Qatar, Bahrain, Oman, Brunei, and Morocco. They also used to exist in Iraq, Libya, Yemen, Iran and Egypt. The new regimes of most of these countries, which abolished monarchies, are worse than the previous ones because they are controlled by self-imposed dictators who are military tyrants at the same time. In as much as Islam denounces the concept of monarchy, it abhors that of dictatorship, military rule, and marital law.

- Islam is NOT and will not agree to the following social, economic and political systems: communist, socialistic, nationalistic, democratic, capitalistic, and totalitarianism.

48

The Islamic system of government is Islam, and it cannot tolerate having the foregoing systems within its land. Islam has its unique political, social, economic, educational, and religious systems within the fold of Islamic teachings and ordinances.

- There is NO party system in Islam. Every Muslim is supposed to watch over the ones who administer the affairs of the Muslim Ummah. Whenever mistakes are made every Muslim is supposed to correct them with the power of his hand or his tongue. Every Muslim should also offer his advice and his suggestions, and help to improve the situation of Muslims at large. In this respect Prophet Muhammad (pbuh) said:

  > *Whoever from amongst you see wrong, should change it with the power of his hand; if he cannot, then with his tongue, and if he cannot, then with his heart. This indeed is the weak faith.*

- Muslims are NOT party members of, or an opposition party to any group. They are to play both rules at the same time because their interest is the love and pleasure of Allah and NOT for their own personal motives. Every Muslim is expected to be actively and positively involved in the affairs of the Muslim Ummah. Allah (swt) says in the Qur'an, in Surah Al-'Imran:

  > **And let there be from you a community who invite to goodness, and enjoin right conduct and**

49

forbid indecency. Such are they who are successful.
(3:104)

• Fanaticism does NOT exist in Islam and Islam is
against those who are fanatics. The tradition of Islam is
meant to be simple, easy to apply, realistic and
practical. Islam is built on glad tidings together rather
than warnings. Prophet Muhammad (pbuh) sent two of
his ambassadors to Yemen with the message of glad
tiding: to present Islam in a simple way and to make
things easy for all people.

• Muslims are NOT vocal; they are not radicals, they are
not reactionary; they are not fanatics; and they are not
to be intimidated; they are not dormant, nor are they to
accept any injustice inflicted upon them or on any
other human being. They are not to accept extreme
spiritual involvement or extreme material indulgence.
They are appointed to be a middle nation. In this
respect, Allah says in the Qur'an in Surah Baqarah
(Cow):

> *Thus We have appointed you a middle*
> *community that you may be witnesses against*
> *mankind, and that the Messenger may be a*
> *witness against you... (2:143)*

• In Islam there is NO compulsion in religion. The idea
of forcing or compelling people to accept one's own
religion is totally against the teachings of Islam. The
Qur'an states emphatically that the method of
conversion through compulsion is wrong and should

not be practiced at all. Allah says in Surah Al-Baqarah (the Cow):

> *There shall be no coercion in matters of faith. Distinct has now become the right way from (the way of) error: hence, he who rejects the powers of evil and believes in God has indeed taken hold a support most unfailing, which shall never give way; for God is All Hearing, All-Knowing. (2:256)*

Compulsion necessitates conversion, and the latter necessitates exploitation. All of these methods are contrary to the teachings of Islam. Freedom of religion is one of the foundations of Islam. Accordingly, Christians and Jews flourished and prospered in the Muslim lands throughout the history of Islam.

- The idea of assassination of innocent people is totally against the teachings of Islam. Islam does not agree or allow any person to follow the method of killing others because of personal differences. To have differences among people is a sign of vitality, dynamism, and healthy atmosphere. When a person kills another person, it is as if he has killed all the people in the world. In this regard, Allah (swt) says in the Qur'an in Surah Al-Ma-idah

> *Because of this did We ordain unto the children of Israel that if anyone slays a human -- unless it be (in punishment) for murder or for spreading corruption on earth-- it shall be as though he did*

slain all mankind; whereas, if anyone saves a life it shall be as though he had saved the lives of all mankind (5:32).

Anyone who kills any innocent person should have capital punishment imposed upon him, and a ransom be paid to the family of the deceased.

- A military coup d'etat is against the teachings of Islam. Prophet Muhammad (pbuh) never caused a coup in his entire life history. It took him thirteen years in Makkah to make a social change in the society, and it also took him another ten years in Madinah before he was able to change the society from a pagan one into a God-fearing one.

The revolution (if one is to use this term) that the Prophet brought about was through evolution. He had to work hard in order to change the personality and character of the individuals and the society. That type of change brought by the Prophet was socially, culturally, morally, religiously, educationally, and politically oriented.

When people were ready to live and practice the change that was brought to them, both privately and publicly, the new system was ready to take over. And indeed, Muslims did take over Makkah and then Islam spread all over Arabia.

- There is no fundamentalism in Islam. It has to do with Christianity as Webster Dictionary explained. If fundamentalism means to follow the fundamental teachings of Islam, then every Muslim is a fundamentalist. But to be dogmatic, radical and evangelic is against the teachings of Islam. Islam condemns all types of extremism. On the other hand, Islam teaches its followers to act as shock-absorbents to most of the activities in life. Otherwise, they are the losers in this part of the world and in the hereafter.

- There is no Holy War in Islam. The word "holy" is a Crusader's terminology. The same thing for a war. Islam will never wage a war against Christians or Jews because they are People of the Book, who have privileges and rights. However, the word Jihad has nothing to do with Holy War. The reader is requested to read more about it in this book.

In the name of Allah, the most Merciful, the Ever Merciful

XI. BUILDING A BETTER FUTURE

In this chapter there is a list of approaches that can be followed in order to build a better future between the Muslims and the non-Muslims.

- **American Government**

    The American government is to recognize the presence of Islam and Muslims as an asset to the future success of America and its civilization. The American government should realize that the problems created in the Middle East will not be solved until the American Muslims are involved in policy-making, peace- creating, and justice for all.

    The White House should recruit a group of American Muslims to Act as a council of advisors to the White House concerning Muslim affairs in America, as well as the affairs of the Muslim world.

- **State Department**

    The State Department should recruit some American Muslims and appoint them as ambassadors, consul generals or other echelons to be sent to some Muslim countries.

- **Political Leaders**

    American foreign policy makers should recognize that democracy of the West is a man-made system. There is no uniformity among those who believe that democracy is the best for the welfare of humanity.

(a) In USA, the commander in-chief is the President, and not the chief of Staff

(b) The democracy of England has monarchy as a symbol, while the exact chief of commander is the Prime Minister.

(c) In Canada, the Prime Minister is the commander in-chief. They don't have President.

(d) In Israel, India, and other countries, the Prime Minister is the ruling person for that country, and not the President.

American leaders, and the West should recognize that capitalism is not the best solution to the betterment of humanity. It is a system whereby the rich exploits the destiny of the people. Through the economic system of capitalism, many people become jobless and homeless. The crime rate, drug abuse, vandalism, and family break-ups have increased tremendously, while the family values have deteriorated.

American leaders should stop helping Israel and the Arab leaders. They should be left to solve their problems by themselves. American leadership should concentrate on their local problems and try to solve them before it is too late for the existence of America as a super power.

- **Press Secretary**

Press Secretary should inform the mass media to be fair with all Americans and treat them equally. They should not correlate American Muslims with any Muslim countries. Muslims of America are Americans – they have already demonstrated their love and respect to America; they have contributed to the success of America and have improved America's image nationally and internationally.

- **Department of Education**

    The Department of Education should recruit American Muslim intellectuals to help in writing those chapters about Islam in text books for the public schools system. The Department of Education should recognize that there are more than half-a-million Muslim students from different foreign countries in different academic institutions. If they are welcomed, absorbed and treated with fairness, they will become the best spokesperson for America in their home countries.

- **Religious Groups**

    The Religious leaders of America have a moral obligation to build bridges of understanding among all the faithful and the God-fearing people. The National Council of Christians and Jews (NCCJ) should include other religious groups and especially the American Muslims. Instead of being called NCCJ, it should be called the American Interfaitth Council (AIC).

    In as much as Christian and Jewish religious leaders are invited for invocations, Muslim religious leaders should also be invited for the same. The Religious leaders should strop accusing Islam and Muslims during their sermons. They should bring the commonalities among all the religious people in the world and especially those who are living in America. Dialogues and trialogues should be initiated among the leaders of the Abrahamic religions. Field trips should be conducted among their religious groups to visit other religious centers to observe and to learn about others. Workshops and training programs should be conducted as well.

- **American Muslims**

    American Muslims have reacted nobly whenever crisis takes place in any Muslim country. They act as "shock absorbers." If the American leadership does not absorb them, they may lose them. Some may react negatively and be extremist as we have seen in some Muslim countries.

    Since freedom of religion is one of the main cardinals of the American Constitution, and since Christians and Jews have acquired their religious freedom on Saturdays and Sunday, Muslims who wish to observe their Friday congregation prayer should be given the freedom to do so without being penalized. Muslims of America are to continue to improve the American civilization through education, knowledge, science, technology and culture.

    Muslims are to be allowed to present their history, their culture and civilization to the American non-Muslims using the TV, radio and newspapers. Muslims are to invite non-Muslims to dialogues for better understanding and for a better future to all. Muslims are to be involved in politics and to assume leadership positions to serve all Americans, irrespective of color, race, creed, nationality or ethnic background.

- **America and the West**

    People in America and the West will continue to suffer with their social, political, economic and moral values until they recognize Islam. They will never improve their values and standards until they follow Islamic teachings. It is only after they benefit from Islam that they will solve many of their contemporary problems.

The people in the West should read what other Western philosophers have said about Islam, so as to benefit from the Islamic teachings. George Bernard Shaw, a Western thinker and philosopher said:

Europe shall declare the Islamic Creed innocent of what men of Europe of the Middle Ages accused it of in evil tales. The religion of Muhammad shall be the system on which the bases of the world peace and happiness shall be established. The solution of the world problems will depend on its philosophy. Many of my compatriots and other Europeans follow the principles of Islam. Therefore, I can prophesy that the European Islamic era is undoubtedly very near.

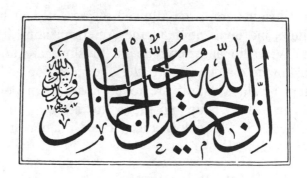

Allah is Beautiful; He like Beauty
(The Prophet says the truth)

XII. BENEFITS OF BECOMING A MUSLIM

A. General

This section is designed for those who wish to become Muslims as to what would be their benefits after accepting Islam. It should be stated here that we are not trying to entice people to become Muslims, nor are we trying to convert them into the folds of Islam. Any person who wishes to become Muslim should recognize that he will get all these benefits and many more. However, he should realize that he has to earn them by trying to practice the teaching of Islam. Practicing the teachings of Islam is as important as believing in it.

B. Benefits

The following items are some of the benefits to be earned and to be enjoyed by those who wish to become Muslims:

1. As far as the Creator (whose proper name is Allah) is concerned, you will be able to identify Him and get to know Him, His role and your relationship to Him. Through His Ninety- Nine Beautiful names, you will be able to communicate with Him any time, 24 hours a day throughout the whole year. As a result of this category, you will be able to know your origin, your root, and the wisdom as to why you are on this planet. You will be able to have good answers to the questions why, how, when, where, what, and other philosophical questions.

2. As a result of the first benefit, your loyalty, allegiance, and obedience will be to the Creator Himself. You will transcend yourself from all types of allegiance to this world. This means that if there is a conflict of interest between your boss, your job, your government, your system or any worldly relationship with the Creator, you will undoubtedly put your trust in Allah,

the Creator of the universe. You will follow Him before you follow anyone else.

3. As a result of the second benefit, you will be able to acquire peace, harmony, tranquility and happiness within yourself, with your family, with people of the world, with the environment and with the universe. One has to remember that the source of peace is Allah, and one of His Beautiful Names is that He is The Peace.

4. As an endorsement to category number three, you will get rid of the extra electrostatic charges from your brain and the CNS by performing the daily Salat. Through Salat you are to prostrate by putting your forehead to the floor; and as such you are grounding yourself, and you are discharging these extra charges into the ground. As a result of this act, you will get rid of many of the neurological diseases from the body.

5. As a result of category four, you will acquire a pleasant personality. You will be friendly and amicable. You would not need to drink alcohol, to use drugs or to get involved in vulgarity or immorality.

6. Through the experience of fasting in Islam, you will be able to have self-control, self-restraint, self-discipline, self-education, self-evaluation, and self-obedience to the Creator Allah. You undoubtedly will be able to improve your health and your personality, character and behavior.

7. As a result of category six, you will be able to control your lusts, selfishness, desires, greed, ego and conceitedness.

8. Another side reaction of category six and seven is that you will be generous and hospitable. You will try to purify yourself and your mistakes by sharing your happiness and your wealth with those who are less fortunate than you. Your rewards will be manifolds, compounded daily until the Day of Judgment.

9. By performing a pilgrimage to Makkah, you will transcend yourself from being nationalistic, sectarian, or denominational into being universal. You will be a part and an essential constituent of the Rainbow of Islam. You will be also part of the Brotherhood of Islam with those who already submitted themselves to the Creator. At the same time, you will get rid (if there is any) of the inferiority or superiority complex. You will also find yourself in synchrony and harmony with all the Prophets and Messengers of Allah since the creation of Adam and Eve until the last and final Messenger to mankind, namely Prophet Muhammad. While in Makkah, you will be able to visit the places of revelations of the Qur'an as well as the places visited by Prophet Abraham and members of his family, namely Hagar and Ishmael. You will visit the First House of Worship to God on earth, namely the Ka'bah. More so, you will visit the place where the first astronauts landed on earth, namely Adam and Eve.

10. In becoming a Muslim, you will do your best to stop all types of exploitations in all their forms: economical, biological, mental, spiritual, psychological, political, etc. You will also take the initiative to liberate people and give them freedom of worship, freedom of speech, and freedom of expression. You will be a leader to lead people to peace, tranquility and happiness.

11. In accepting Islam, you will help to reduce all types of social ills in the society: juvenile delinquency, child abuse, women's battering, incest, homosexuality, sexual promiscuity, premarital relationships, extramarital relationships, and other vices.

12. As a benefit of category eleven, you will reduce and eliminate venereal diseases, AIDS, and other diseases of similar nature in the society.

13. Finally, when you die, you will die at peace. You will have a happy life in the grave and later an eternal happiness. Angels at the time of death will welcome you, and those in the grave will comfort you. They will also show you your place in Paradise. In the Day of Judgment, you will be able to see and meet the Creator, Allah, the Merciful. You will be able to see and meet all the Prophets and Messengers of God to mankind including Noah, Abraham, Moses, Jesus and Muhammad. You will be able to see and meet any and all of your friends and relatives. You will live an eternal life of bliss in Paradise.

C. Concluding Remarks

It should be mentioned here that these benefits and many more cannot be purchased with money anywhere in the world. No one is to sell them to you or to advertise them on TV. You have to take the initiative yourself and try to acquire them by accepting Islam first, and then by practicing its teachings. You should be honest with yourself, sincere, and truthful to the Creator. You should try wholeheartedly to practice what you believe, regardless of whether someone else is good or not.

While seeking happiness is a must, it should not be measured with other people's standards or with material gains. Happiness is from within yourself, and it should be transformed from its potential to its kinetic forms. People around you should feel your happiness as well as benefit from you. If so, the question is to be raised: are you ready to accept the challenge as of today? Remember! Tomorrow may not come, and it will be too late. Welcome aboard! And we wish you a good and a happy life.

XIII. FINAL REMARKS

At last, it has become imperative that people should stop accusing others. People should eliminate all types of prejudices and start to understand and to respect one another. It is only through understanding and communication that people will try to live in peace and harmony. Non-Muslims should recognize that they are no more living in medieval ages, but in the twenty-first century. People are using satellites across the globe so that they will get to know each other better.

To understand Islam and Muslims in the right perspective will help improve relationships, reduce friction, and build better bridges of cooperation for all. People do need to work together so that the new generations from all of us will live a happy life; otherwise, we will be blamed by them, and we will be punished on the Day of Judgement for not taking the initiative. We have a golden opportunity in our hands, and it is better to seize it before it is too late.

Might should not be considered to be right, rather right is might. Those nations that think they are mighty because of military power should be condemned if they use their power to subjugate other nations. They should remember Pharaoh, people of 'Aad, Thamood, Salih , Loot, Noah, and others. All were destroyed.

Allah is the Greatest!

XIV. ISLAMIC EXPRESSIONS

Muslims throughout the world have learned from childhood to use certain expressions in their daily lives. These expressions are taken either from the Qur'an and/or from the Sunnah. Muslims do use these phrases irrespective of their nationality, ethnic background or language.

It is strange enough that an Arab Muslim going out from Makkah in Arabia to anywhere in the world, will find himself at home with the other Muslims. The same religious expressions, the same phrases, and the same sentences are used without difficulty to understand one another.

These expressions are used in writing as well as in verbal communication. These phrases have made the Muslims appreciate their religious values and teachings. Muslims find it easy to use such expressions since many of them cannot be translated easily without finding a series of sentences to explain them. Non-Muslims who associate themselves with Muslims find it difficult to understand these phrases, sentences, and expressions. Many times the general understanding of the talk is lost due to the lack of knowledge for the meaning of such expressions.

This section is meant to explain some of the major expressions in a simple language where non-Muslims will communicate with Muslims with better understanding. It is only through communication with the proper words, sentences, phrases, expressions, and paragraphs that people may realize how friendly and respectful they are to one another. The following is a partial list of these expressions.

A'uzu Billahi Minashaitanir Rajim

This is an expression and a statement that Muslims have to recite before reading the Qur'an, before speaking, before doing any work, before making a supplication, before taking ablution, before entering the wash room, and before doing many other daily activities. The meaning of the phrase is: "I seek refuge in Allah from the outcast Satan". Allah is the Arabic name of God.

Satan (Shaitan) is the source of evil and he always tries to misguide and mislead people. The Qur'an states that Satan is not an angel but a member of the Jinn, which are spiritual beings created by Allah. So the belief that Satan is a fallen angel is rejected in Islam.

Bismillahir Rahmanir Rahim

This is a phrase from the Qur'an that is recited before reading the Qur'an. It is to be read immediately after one reads the phrase. "A'uzu Billahi Minash-Shaitanir Rajim".

This phrase is also recited before doing any activity. The meaning of it is: "In the name of Allah, the Most Beneficent, the Most Merciful".

Al-Hamdu Lillahi Rabbil Alamin

This is a verse from Qur'an that Muslims recite and say many times per day. Other than being recited daily during prayers, a Muslims reads this expression in every activity of his daily life. The meaning of it is *"Praise be to Allah, the Lord of the worlds."* Before he does his daily work; and when he finishes, he thanks Allah for His favors. A Muslim is grateful to Allah for all His blessings. It is a statement of thanks, appreciation, and gratitude from the creature to his Creator.

Muhammadun Rasulullah

This statement is the second part of the first pillar of Islam. Its meaning is: "Muhammad is the Messenger of Allah".

The other part of the first pillar is *"There is no lord but Allah"*. The meaning of the second part is that Prophet Muhammad is the last and final prophet and messenger of Allah to mankind. He is the culmination, summation, and purification of the previous prophets of Allah to humanity. A Muslim says this statement many times everyday.

Allahu Akbar

Muslims say this statement numerous times. During the call for prayer, during prayer, when they are happy, and wish to express their approval of what they hear, when they slaughter an animal, and when they want to praise a speaker, Muslims do say this expression of Allahu Akbar. Actually, it is the most said expression in the world. Its meaning: "Allah is the Greatest". Muslims praise Allah in every aspect of life; and as such they say Allahu Akbar.

Subhanahu Wa Ta'ala

This is an expression that Muslims use whenever the name or Allah is pronounced or written. The meaning of this expression is "Allah is pure of having partners and He is exalted from having a son". Muslims believe that Allah is the only God, the Creator of the Universe. He does not have partners or children.

Sometimes, Muslims use some other expressions when the name of Allah is written or pronounced. Some of which are:

"'Azza Wa Jall": He is the Mighty and the Majestic.
"Jalla Jalaluh": He is the Exalted Majestic.

Sadaqallahul 'Azim

This is a statement of truth that a Muslim says after reading any amount of verses from the Qur'an. The meaning of it is: "Allah says the truth".

The Qur'an is the exact words of Allah in verbatim. When Allah speaks, He says the truth, and when the Qur'an is being recited, a Muslim is reciting the words of truth of Allah. Hence, he says: "Sadaqa Allah Al-'Azim".

Sallallahu 'Alaihi Wa Sallam

This is an expression that Muslims us whenever the name of Prophet Muhammad (s.a.w.) is mentioned or written. The meaning of it is: *"May the blessing and the peace of Allah be upon Him (Muhammad)"*. Another expression that is alternative used is:

"'Alaihissalatu Wassalam". This expression means: "On him (Muhammad) are the blessings and the peace (of Allah)".

Allah has ordered Muslims, in the Qur'an, to say such an expression. Muslims are informed that if they proclaim such a statement once, Allah will reward them ten times.

Radhiallahu 'Anhu

This is an expression to be used by Muslims whenever a name of a companion of the Prophet (s.a.w.) is mentioned or used in writing. The meaning of this statement is: "May Allah be pleased with him".

Muslims are taught to be respectful to the elderly, to the leaders, and to those who contributed to the spread and success of Islam. They are to be grateful to the companions of the Prophet (s.a.w.) for their sacrifices, their leadership, and their contributions. Muslims are advised to use this phrase when such names are mentioned or written.

Assalamu 'Alaikum

This is an expression that Muslims say whenever they meet one another. It is a statement of greeting with peace. The meaning of it is: *"Peace be upon you"*.

Muslims try to establish peace on earth even through the friendly relation of greeting and meeting one another. The other forms are: *"Assalamu 'Alaikum Wa Rahmatullah"*, which means: "May the peace and the mercy of Allah be upon you, and "Assalamu 'Alaikum Wa Rahmatullahi Wa Barakatuh", which means: "May the peace, the mercy, and the blessing of Allah be upon you".

Wa 'Alaikumus Salam

This is an expression that a Muslim is to say as an answer for the greeting. When a person greets another with a salutation of peace, the answer for the greeting is an answer of peace. The meaning of this statement is: "And upon you is the peace". The other expressions are: *"Wa 'Alaikums Salam Wa Rahmatullah"*. And "Wa 'Alaikums Salam Wa Rahmatullahi Wa Barakatuh".

Jazakallah Khayran

This is a statement of thanks and appreciation to be said to the person who does a favor. Instead of saying "thanks" (Shukran), the Islamic statement of thanks is to say this phrase. Its meaning is: "May Allah reward you for the good".

It is understood that human beings can't repay one another enough. Hence, it is better to request Almighty Allah to reward the person who did a favor and to give him the best.

In Sha' Allah

When a person wishes to plan for the future, when he promises, when he makes resolutions, and when he makes a pledge, he makes them with the permission and the will of Allah. For this reason, a Muslim uses the Qur'anic instructions by saying "Insha'Allah". The meaning of this statement is: "If Allah wills".

Muslims are to strive hard and to put their trusts with Allah. They leave the results in the Hands of Allah.

Ma Sha'Allah

This is an expression that Muslims say whenever they are excited and surprised. When they wish to express their happiness, they use such an expression. The meaning of "Ma Sha'Allah" is: "Whatever Allah wants". Or: "Whatever Allah wants to give, He gives". This means that whenever Allah gives something good to someone, blesses him, honors him, and opens the door of success in business, a Muslim says this statement of "Ma Sha'Allah".

Inna Lillahi Wa Inna Ilaihi Raji'un

When a Muslim is struck with a calamity, when he loses one of his loved ones, or when he has gone bankrupt, he should be patient and say this statement, the meaning of which is: "We are from Allah and to Him we are returning".

Muslims believe that Allah is the One Who gives and it is He Who takes away. He is testing us. Hence, a Muslim submits himself to Allah. He is grateful and thankful to Allah for whatever he gets. On the other hand, he is patient and says this expression in times of turmoil and calamity.

La Hawla Wa La Quwwata Illa Billah

The meaning of this expression is; *"There is no power and no strength save in Allah"*. This expression is read by a Muslim when he is struck by a calamity, or is taken over by a situation beyond his control. A Muslim puts his trust into the Hands of Allah, and submits himself to Allah.

Astaghfirullah

This is an expression used by a Muslim when he wants to ask Allah forgiveness. The meaning of it is: "I ask Allah forgiveness".

A Muslim says this phrase many times, even when he is talking to another person. When a Muslim abstains from doing wrong, or even when he wants to prove that he is innocent of an incident, he uses this expression of "Astaghfirullah". After every Salah (prayer), a Muslim says this statement three times.

Barakallah

This is an expression, which means: "May the blessings of Allah (be upon you)". When a Muslim wants to thank another person, he uses different statements to express his thanks, appreciation, and gratitude. One of them is to say "Baraka Allah".

Chart of Daily *Salah*

FAJR	2 SUNNAH	2 FARD
ZUHR	2 SUNNAH	4 FARD
'ASR	4 FARD	---
MAGHRIB	3 FARD	2 SUNNAH
'ISHA	4 FARD	2 SUNNAH and 3 WITR

71

INVOCATION

City Of Diamond Bar

Dr. Ahmad H. Sakr, Director

September 18, 2001

Your Honor the Mayor Mr. Robert Huff
Your Excellencies the Members of the City Council
The Honorable members of the Sheriff & Fire Departments
The Respected Delegates and Representatives of the Community Leaders
The Respected Religious Leaders

Ladies and Gentlemen:

We came here to share with you our sorrows, and especially the sorrows of those families who lost their loved ones. We pray to You O God Almighty to bring peace, justice, and happiness to all of us. We also pray to God to revenge from the criminals who committed such cowardly acts in New York and Washington DC. Anyone who kills an innocent person as if he killed humanity at large; and anyone who saves the life of one person as if he saved the life of humanity. Moreover, anyone who brings commotion and trouble to the society is committing a bigger sin than killing. O God! You are the Most Merciful, the Most Compassionate, the Creator of the whole universe. We are Your creation. You Created us to live in peace and harmony. One of the Beautiful Names of Yours is Assalam. This means that You are the Source of Peace. Please O God, help us all and guide us all, to control our agonies, distress and emotions. Please Our Lord, help us to bring peace and harmony among all of us irrespective of race, color, nationality, language, creed, or religion. We are all Your servants and the children of Adam and Eve.

Please Almighty God: Help us to understand the difference between those who committed the crime and Religion! Help us not to associate any crime with any community, society, or any country, or any religion. Our Lord! Help us to understand each other without being biased or prejudiced! Help us and guide us to communicate and to Dialogue with each other.

Ladies and Gentlemen:

Yes! Almighty God! You have put in our brains so many things that are common to each other. Therefore, Almighty God! Help us to Dialogue in each other on commonalties rather than on differences. Yes! O God! Ignorance is one of the major crises in every society.

We came here to share our sorrows and agonies! We came here to find the means and methods for building a better society for all of us...You are the Most Merciful, Please shower us with your mercy now and forever, Ameen. God Bless you all, and God Bless America. Ameen.

Pillars of Iman

The Belief In:

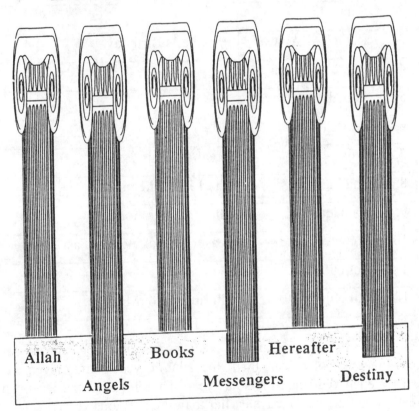

Allah

Angels

Books

Messengers

Hereafter

Destiny

Lunar Calendar

In as much as the Gregorian year starts with January and ends up with December, the Islamic Lunar Calendar goes like this.

	Name of the Month	Occasions
1.	Muharram	New Year; 'Ashura
2.	Safar	
3.	Rabie' Al-Awwal	Prophet's Birthday
4.	Rabie Al-Thani	
5.	Jamadi Al-Awwal	
6.	Jamdi Al-Thani	
7.	Rajab	Israa'/ Mi'raj
8.	Sha'ban	The 15th of the month
9.	Ramadan	The Fasting month
10.	Shawwal	Feast of Breaking the Fast
11.	Zul Qi'dah	
12.	Zul Hijjah	Pilgrimage to Makkah.

Since the Lunar Calendar year is 354 days, i.e. eleven days less than the solar year, then the Islamic year starts eleven days earlier each year than the solar year. Therefore, all the feasts and festivities fall eleven days earlier than the previous year.

Days of the Week

English	Arabic	Meanings
1. Sunday	Al-Ahad	The First
2. Monday	Al-Ithnain	The Second
3. Tuesday	Al-Thulaatha'	The Third
4. Wednesday	Al-Arbia'a'	The Fourth
5 Thursday	Al-Khamees	The Fifth
6. Friday *	Al-Jumu'ah	The Sixth
7. Saturday	Al-Sabt	The Seventh

*   Friday is a holiday and a sacred day. Muslims are to congregate in a mosque, and   offer their group prayers. The religious leader (Imam) is to give a sermon (Khutbah), and then lead the believers in prayer. This type of obligatory prayer is to be held at noon time. Muslims are to close their shops, offices, and schools so as to attend the Friday prayer called Salatul-Jumu`ah.

Eid Chanting
(Takaabir Al-Eid)

During the two feasts: Eidul-Fitr and Eidul-Adha, Muslims are recommended to recite the chanting of these Eids. Muslims are to glorify Allah for one day for Eidul-Fitr or four days for Eidul-Adha. The chanting goes like this:

Allahu Akbar, Allahu Akbar, Allahu Akbar
La ilaha illa-L-Lah

Allahu Akbar, Allahu Akbar, Wa lil-Lahi L-hamd

Allahu Akbar Kabeera, wa-L- hamdu li-L-Lahi kathera
Wa subhana-L-lahi bukratan wa aseela

La ilaha ila-l-lahu, wahdah, sadaqa wa'adah
Wa nasara 'abdah
Wa a' azza jundahu, wa hazama-l-ahzaba wahdah

La ilaha ila-l-lah, wa la na'budu illa iyyah
Mukhliseena lahu-d-deena wa law kariha-l-kafiroon

Allahumma salli 'ala sayyidina Muhammad
Wa 'ala ali Sayyidina Muhammad
Wa 'ala ashabi sayyidina Muhammad
Wa 'ala ansari sayyidina Muhammad
Wa 'ala azwaji sayyidina Muhammad
Wa 'ala dhurriyati sayyidina Muhammad
Wasallim tasleeman katheera

Allah is the Greatest, Allah is the Greatest, Allah is the Greatest. There is no deity but Allah.

Allah is the Greatest, Allah is the Greatest,
Praise be to Allah.

Allah is Greatest. The powerful and abundant praises are due to Allah, and Glory be to Allah in the morning and in the evening

There is no deity but Allah the One and only, He fulfilled His promise, helped His servant, strengthened His forces, and alone routed out the clans.

There is no deity but Allah, Him alone we   worship, offering Him sincere devotion even if the disbelievers distaste (it).

O Allah! Evoke Your blessings on Prophet Muhammad, the family of Prophet Muhammad, the companions of Prophet Muhammad, the helpers of Prophet Muhammad, the wives of Prophet Muhammad, and the descendants of Prophet Muhammad,
O Allah! Do send abundant peace on the Prophet.

Praise be to Allah, the Lord of the worlds.

Sample of Prayer Time Table

Muslims are to pray five times a day through the whole year. The times of the prayers move from one day to another by a minute or two upward or downward depending on the season. Attached is a sample of a Time Table of prayer for one month in a specific year and for a specific location.

Glory to (Allah) who did take His Servant for a journey by night from the Sacred Mosque to the farthest Mosque whose precints we did bless,-in order that we might show him some of our Signs: for He is the One who heareth and seeth (all things).

مُبْحَنَ ٱلَّذِىٓ أَسْرَىٰ بِعَبْدِهِۦ لَيْلًا مِّنَ ٱلْمَسْجِدِ ٱلْحَرَامِ إِلَى ٱلْمَسْجِدِ ٱلْأَقْصَا ٱلَّذِى بَٰرَكْنَا حَوْلَهُۥ لِنُرِيَهُۥ مِنْ ءَايَٰتِنَآ إِنَّهُۥ هُوَ ٱلسَّمِيعُ ٱلْبَصِيرُ ۞

October 2001

Sunday	Monday	Tuesday	Wednesday	Thursday	Friday	Saturday
	1 Rajab 14 05:23 06:46 12:41 04:03 06:40 07:58	**2** Rajab 15 05:23 06:47 12:41 04:02 06:39 07:57	**3** Rajab 16 05:24 06:48 12:40 04:01 06:37 07:56	**4** Rajab 17 05:25 06:48 12:40 04:00 06:36 07:54	**5** Rajab 18 05:26 06:49 12:40 03:59 06:34 07:53	**6** Rajab 19 05:26 06:50 12:39 03:58 06:33 07:52
7 Rajab 20 05:27 06:51 12:39 03:57 06:32 07:50	**8** Rajab 21 05:28 06:51 12:39 03:56 06:31 07:49	**9** Rajab 22 05:29 06:52 12:39 03:55 06:29 07:48	**10** Rajab 23 05:29 06:53 12:38 03:54 06:28 07:46	**11** Rajab 24 05:30 06:54 12:38 03:53 06:27 07:45	**12** Rajab 25 05:31 06:54 12:38 03:52 06:25 07:44	**13** Rajab 26 05:32 06:55 12:38 03:52 06:24 07:43
14 Rajab 27 05:32 06:56 12:37 03:51 06:23 07:41	**15** Rajab 28 05:33 06:57 12:37 03:50 06:22 07:40	**16** Rajab 29 05:34 06:58 12:37 03:49 06:20 07:39	**17** Rajab 30 05:35 06:58 12:37 03:48 06:19 07:38	**18** Sha'ban 1 05:35 06:59 12:37 03:47 06:18 07:37	**19** Sha'ban 2 05:36 07:00 12:36 03:46 06:17 07:36	**20** Sha'ban 3 05:37 07:01 12:36 03:45 06:16 07:35
21 Sha'ban 4 05:38 07:02 12:36 03:44 06:14 07:33	**22** Sha'ban 5 05:38 07:03 12:36 03:43 06:13 07:32	**23** Sha'ban 6 05:39 07:03 12:36 03:43 06:12 07:31	**24** Sha'ban 7 05:40 07:04 12:36 03:42 06:11 07:30	**25** Sha'ban 8 05:41 07:05 12:36 03:41 06:10 07:29	**26** Sha'ban 9 05:41 07:06 12:35 03:40 06:09 07:28	**27** Sha'ban 10 05:42 07:07 12:35 03:39 06:08 07:27
28 Sha'ban 11 04:43 06:08 11:35 02:39 05:07 06:27	**29** Sha'ban 12 04:44 06:09 11:35 02:38 05:06 06:26	**30** Sha'ban 13 04:45 06:09 11:35 02:37 05:05 06:25	**31** Sha'ban 14 04:45 06:10 11:35 02:36 05:04 06:24	In the Name of Allah, The Beneficent, The Merciful **ISLAMIC EDUCATION CENTER** 659 Brea Canyon Rd. #2, / Walnut Ca. 91789 USA Phone: (909) 594-1310 Fax: (909) 444-0832		

Walnut, California

Communications

UNITED STATES CONFERENCE OF CATHOLIC BISHOPS

Catholic Bishops and Muslim Leaders Issue Joint Statement

WASHINGTON (September 14, 2001) -- Catholic Bishops and Muslim leaders issued a joint statement today (September 14) in response to this week's terrorist attacks on the United States.

Noting that Catholics and Muslims meet together regularly and engage in many civic projects, the statement says: "We believe that the one God calls us to be peoples of peace. Nothing in our Holy Scriptures, nothing in our understanding of God's revelation, nothing that is Christian or Islamic justifies terrorist acts and disruption of millions of lives which we have witnessed this week. Together we condemn those actions as evil and diametrically opposed to true religion."

This is the full text of the statement:

Catholics and Muslims meet regularly as friends and religious partners in dialogue and engage together in many community projects. We are fully committed to one another as friends, believers, and citizens of this great land. We abhor all terrorist acts and hate crimes and implore all American citizens to refrain from sinking to the mentality and immorality of the perpetrators of Tuesday's (September 11, 2001) crimes.

The U. S. Conference of Catholic Bishops and American Muslim Council, Islamic Circle of North America, Islamic Society of North America, Muslim American Society and numerous Islamic centers and councils have co-sponsored dialogues on religious themes and we commit ourselves to the many noble goals of interreligious cooperation. We believe that the one God calls us to be peoples of peace. Nothing in our Holy Scriptures, nothing in our understanding of God's revelation, nothing that is Christian or Islamic justifies terrorist acts and disruption of millions of lives which we have witnessed this week. Together we condemn those actions as evil and diametrically opposed to true religion.

We urge all American citizens to unify during this national tragedy and encourage cooperation among all ethnic, cultural, racial, and religious groups constituting the mosaic of our society. We appeal to American citizens to come to the assistance of the countless victims of Tuesday's crimes and the victims of any crimes of hate in the aftermath of those awful events. We join in supporting our Government in the pursuit of those who were responsible for Tuesday's terrorist acts, always mindful of the moral imperative to act with restraint and respect for civilian lives. We appeal to law enforcement agencies and the general public to assist those who may be targets of hate crimes. We entreat Catholics and Muslims to join together and with all people of good will in services of prayer and community programs promoting peace.

Most Rev. Tod D. Brown
Bishop of Orange
Chairman, Bishops' Committee for
Ecumenical and Interreligious Affairs
U. S. Conference of Catholic Bishops

Dr. Muzammil H. Siddiqi
Director, Islamic Society of Orange County
Islamic Society of North America

Aly R. Abuzaakouk
Executive Director
American Muslim Council

Dr. Sayyid M. Syeed
Secretary General
Islamic Society of North America

Naeem Baig
Secretary General
Islamic Circle of North America

Imam W. D. Mohammed
Muslim American Society

Office of Communications
United States Conference of Catholic Bishops
3211 4th Street, N.E., Washington, DC 20017-1194 (202) 541-3000

September 14, 2001 Copyright © by United States Conference of Catholic Bishops

KNOWLEDGE

Islam emphasizes the importance of knowledge to all mankind. It is only through true knowledge that one can appreciate the Creator of the Universe namely Allah (swt). Muslims are ordained to seek knowledge from cradle to grave and as far as a person can to obtain it.

In as much as seeking knowledge is a must on every Muslim, dissemination of knowledge is also incumbent on Muslims to the members of the society. The methods of disseminating the information should be lawful, as well as the truth is to be released to everyone. Hiding or keeping the true knowledge away from those who seek it, is considered a sin.

The best investment for every human being is through: perpetual charity (Sadaqa Jariya), useful knowledge that people shall benefit or, and a loving child who shall make special prayers for his/her parents.

LEGALITY

The Foundation has been established and registered with the Secretary of the State of Illinois since January 8,1987 as a nonprofit, charitable, educational, religious and /or scientific society within the meaning of section 501 (c) (3) of the Internal Revenue Code.

The Foundation has a tax-exempt status with the IRS, and donations are considered tax-deductible.

FINANCES

The finances of the FOUNDATION are mainly from donations and contributions in the form of cash, assets and wills.

INUMERENT OF INCOME

No part of the net earnings of the Corporation shall inure to the benefit of, or be distributed to, its members, directors, officers or other private persons except that the Corporation shall be authorized and empowered to pay reasonable compensation for services rendered.

PURPOSES

The purposes of the FOUNDATION are summarized as follows:

1. To promote Islamic Knowledge through education.
2. To create a better understanding of Islam among Muslims and non-Muslims through education and communication.
3. To publish books and other literature about Islam and its teachings
4. To disseminate Islamic Knowledge and education through TV, Radio, Video, and other means of mass communications.
5. To establish ecumenical among the religious people of America so that a better understanding will be created.

ACTIVITIES

The activities of the FOUNDATION shall include, but not be limited to the following:

1. Publishing literature pertaining to Islam.
2. Producing audio cassettes and audio-visual tapes on certain topics of Islam.
3. Giving lectures related to Islam as a religion, culture and civilization.
4. Cooperation with other societies, foundations and organizations whose aims and objectives are similar to the FOUNDATION.

KNOWLEDGE IN THE QUR'AN

The word knowledge ('ILM) is mentioned in the Qur'an more than 700 times in 87 different forms. Some of the pertinent Ayat are listed below.

1. The first Ayat revealed to Prophet Muhammad (pbuh) at Cave Hira' are in Surah Al-Alaq (The Clot) (96:1-5). They are related to knowledge of embryology through scientific investigation.

2. Allah honors all those who are knowledgeable. These people cannot be compared with the ignorant ones. See Surah Al-Zumar (The Troops) (35:28)

3. Only the knowledgeable people are those who do appreciate the creations of Allah (swt) . They are the ones who respect Him and worship Him with knowledge and humility. Please read Surah Fatir (The Creator) (35:28)

4. Knowledge is in the Hands of Allah and it is at His disposal. People are to seek the true knowledge from its source namely Allah. Read Surah Al-Mulk (The Sovereignty) (67:26).

5.   People are to seek knowledge from Allah (swt) are to request Him to enrich them daily with 'ILM. Read Surah Taha (20:114).

KNOWLEDGE IN THE HADITH

Prophet Muhammad (pbuh) emphasized 'ILM tremendously and encouraged Muslims to seek knowledge in any part of the world. The following is a summary:

1.   In one Hadith the Prophet says: "The Knowledgeable people ('Ulama) are the inheritors to the Prophets."

2.   In another Hadith He encouraged Muslims to seek knowledge, saying: "Seeking knowledge is a must on every Muslim."

3.   In another place, He demanded that knowledge is to be sought throughout lifetime, saying: "Seek knowledge from cradle to grave."

4.   Knowledge is to be disseminated to all, and the best knowledge is that of the Qur'an, saying: "The best amongst you are the ones who learn Qur'an and teach it to others."

5.   Knowledge is to be taught and to be carried on even after death. In His Hadith the Prophet said: "When a person dies, his deeds are over, except from three things; perpetual charity, a useful knowledge, or a good child who makes supplications for him."

The FOUNDATION will continue, with the help of Almighty God (Allah), to publish more useful literature.

With the generous help of the friends, The Foundation will be able to achieve its purposes, Inshaallah.

For More Information, Please Write To:

Foundation For Islamic Knowledge
P.O. Box 665 Lombard, Illinois 60148 U.S.A.
Phone: (630) 495-4817   Fax (630) 627-8894

PUBLICATIONS

I. BOOKS ON HEALTH, FOOD AND NUTRITION:

1. Dietary Regulations & Food Habits of Muslims
2. Overeating and Behavior
3. Islam on Alcohol
4. Alcohol in Beverages, Drugs, Foods and Vitamins
5. Cheese
6. AFTO and FAO
* 7. Fasting in Islam
8. Food and Overpopulation
9. Honey: Food and a Medicine
* 10. Gelatin
11. Shortening in Foods
12. A Manual on Food Shortenings
* 13. Pork: Possible Reasons for its Prohibition
14. Food Supplementation
15. World Health Organization for Muslim Nations
* 16. A Muslim Guide to Food Ingredients
17. Natural Therapeutics of Medicine in Islam
      (co-authored)
18. Islamic Dietary Laws & Practices (co-authored)
19. Food and Nutrition Manual (co-authored)
20. A Handbook of Muslim Foods
* 21. Understanding Halal Foods: Fallacies and Facts

II. BOOKS ABOUT FRIDAY KHUTAB:

* 1.   Book of Al-Khutab
* 2.   Islamic Orations
* 3.   Orations from the Pulpit
* 4.   Chronicle of Khutab
* 5.   Friday Khutab

* 6. A Manual of Friday Khutab
* 7. Khutab Al-Masjid
* 8. Khutab From Mihrab

III. GENERAL SUBJECTS:

* 1. Islamic Fundamentalism (co-authored)
* 2. Du 'a' After Completing the Recitation of Qur'an
* 3. Introducing Islam to non-Muslims (co-authored)
  4. Prostration – Sujood (new edition)
  5. Guidelines of Employment by Muslim Communities (co-authored)
* 6. Farewell Khutbah of the Prophet – Its Universal Values
* 7. Understanding Islam and Muslims
* 8. Muslims and non-Muslims: Face to Face
* 9. Matrimonial Education in Islam (New Edition)
* 10. Life, Death and the Life After
* 11. The Golden Book of Islamic Lists
* 12. Al-Jinn
* 13. Islam and Muslims: Myth or Reality
  14. Islamic Awareness
* 15. Death and Dying
* 16. Family Values in Islam
* 17. Book of Inquiries
* 18 The Adolescent Life
* 19. Social Services and Counseling
* 20. A Course on Islamic Shari'ah
* 21. Da'wah Through Dialogue
* 22. Understanding the Qur'an
* 23. Themes of the Qur'an
* 24. Book of Knowledge
* 25. Reflections from a Flying Falcon

* 26.   Feasts, Festivities and Holidays

*   These publications are available from:

Foundation for Islamic Knowledge
P.O. Box 665
Lombard, IL 60148
Phone: (630) 495-4817 / Fax: (630) 627-8894

NEWSLETTER

The Foundation has a newsletter called Perspectives, it is published bi-monthly, and distributed free. If you wish to have a copy of the newsletter, please write to the address below.

Virginia Office
(Newsletter/Perspectives)
P. O. Box 65250
Hampton, VA 23665

BOOKS TO BE PUBLISHED

1. Islamic Perspectives
2. Islamic Understanding
3. Islam vs. Muslims
4. The Book of Healing
5. Speakers Bureau Guide Book
6. Health, Hygiene and Nutrition
7. Halal – Haram book of Khutab
8. Book of Du 'a'
9. The Book of Targheeb
10. Scientific Reflections from the Qur'an
11. Biological Terms in the Qur'an
12. Educational Institutions in Islam
13. Writing an Islamic Will
14. Qur'an Commentary in Summary
15. Book of Wisdom
16. Welcome to the World of Islam
17. A Lifetime Journey
18. Arafa of the Hereafter
19. Al-Insaan: The Human Being

These and other books will not be published unless someone like you comes forward and extend a hand of help. You may sponsor any of the above books, or any number of copies of a particular book.

Your help in any capacity is greatly needed even to pay the previous debts to the printers.

The foundation is tax-exempt from the IRS and your donations are tax-deductible. The employer I.D. number with the I.R.S. is 36-352-8916.

For more information, or to send your donation, please contact:

Foundation for Islamic Knowledge
P.O. Box 665, Lombard, IL 60148,USA
Phone: (630) 495-4817 / Fax: (630) 627-8894

بِسْمِ اللَّهِ الرَّحْمَٰنِ الرَّحِيمِ

اقْرَأْ بِاسْمِ رَبِّكَ الَّذِى خَلَقَ ۞ خَلَقَ الْإِنسَٰنَ مِنْ عَلَقٍ ۞ اقْرَأْ وَرَبُّكَ الْأَكْرَمُ ۞ الَّذِى عَلَّمَ بِالْقَلَمِ ۞ عَلَّمَ الْإِنسَٰنَ مَا لَمْ يَعْلَمْ ۞

In the name of Allah, Most Gracious, Most Merciful.
Read! In the name of your Lord and Cherisher who created,
Created man out of a clot.
Read! And your Lord is Most Bountiful,
He who taught the use of the pen,
Taught man that which he knew not.